Teaching Study Skills and Strategies in Grades 4–8

Related Titles of Interest

Teaching Study Skills and Strategies in College
Patricia Iannuzzi, Stephen S. Strichart, and Charles T. Mangrum II
ISBN: 0-205-26817-X

Active Learning: 101 Strategies to Teach Any Subject
Mel Silberman
ISBN: 0-205-17866-9

Teaching Study Skills and Strategies in High School
Stephen S. Strichart, Charles T. Mangrum II, and Patricia Iannuzzi
ISBN: 0-205-19881-3

Teaching Study Strategies to Students with Learning Disabilities
Stephen S. Strichart and Charles T. Mangrum II
ISBN: 0-205-13992-2

For more information or to purchase a book, please call 1-800-278-3525.

Teaching Study Skills and Strategies in Grades 4–8

CHARLES T. MANGRUM II
University of Miami

PATRICIA IANNUZZI
Florida International University

STEPHEN S. STRICHART
Florida International University

Allyn and Bacon
Boston London Toronto Sydney Tokyo Singapore

Internet: www.abacon.com
America Online: keyword: College Online

Some of the activities in this book have been adapted from *Teaching Study Strategies to Students with Learning Disabilities* by Stephen S. Strichart and Charles T. Mangrum II and published by Allyn & Bacon, 1993.

Library of Congress Cataloging-in-Publication Data

Mangrum, Charles T.
Teaching study skills and strategies in grades 4–8 / Charles T. Mangrum II. Patricia Iannuzzi. Stephen S. Strichart.
p. cm.
Include bibliographical references.
ISBN 0-205-19879-1
1. Study skills—Handbooks, manuals, etc. 2. Note-taking—Handbooks, manuals, etc. 3. Research—Handbooks, manuals, etc. 4. School children—Handbooks, manuals, etc. I. Iannuzzi, Patricia. II. Strichart, Stephen S. III. Title.
LB1601.M26 1998
371.3′028′1—DC21 97-13470
CIP

Printed in the United States of America
10 9 8 7 6 5 4 3 2 1 01 00 99 98 97

Contents

Introduction

HOW THIS BOOK WILL HELP

This book provides opportunities for active learning in the classroom. The reproducible activities will help students master study skills and strategies important for success in many subject areas. Teaching students to use study skills and strategies effectively is an important step in transforming dependent learners into independent learners. The activities are designed to help students become independent learners in an increasingly technology-based learning environment.

Accompanying this book is a trial version of a computer assessment titled Study Skills and Strategies Assessment—Grades Four through Eight (3S–Gr 4–8). 3S–Gr 4–8 assesses students' use of the study skills and strategies taught in this book. The free trial disk, available in Windows only, allows you to administer 3S–Gr 4–8 to five students. You may then purchase a disk with either 50 or an unlimited number of administrations in either Windows or Macintosh versions. The order form is found at the end of this book.

THE STUDY SKILLS AND STRATEGIES OF STUDENTS IN GRADES 4–8

Many authors have described the study skills and strategies of students in grades 4–8. When summarized, their conclusions are that many students:

1. do not know how to organize their study time and space and use good study habits to maximize their opportunity for learning.
2. do not have a system for taking notes from class presentations.
3. have underdeveloped study strategies for obtaining, organizing, and recording important information from textbooks.
4. do not make use of the visual aids found in textual materials.
5. have little knowledge of effective techniques useful for remembering information learned from teachers and textual materials.

6. do not know how to prepare for and take the common forms of tests administered in school.
7. do not know how to read, interpret, and solve math word problems in a systematic manner.
8. are not sufficiently familiar with print, electronic, and other sources of information found in today's library.
9. do not make adequate use of reference books and other sources of information that can further enhance their learning.
10. have incomplete knowledge on how to do library research and write a research paper.

STUDY SKILLS AND STRATEGIES TAUGHT IN THIS BOOK

The study skills and strategies taught in this book are those most important for success in grades 4–8. The study skills and strategies are presented in the following eleven chapters.

Chapter 1. Using Study Time, Habits, Space

Students have many demands on their time. They must make effective use of their time to complete school assignments and prepare adequately for tests. Students need good study habits to get good grades. They must also have a good place to study. In this chapter students are taught strategies for scheduling their time, evaluating and improving their study habits, and organizing their study space.

Chapter 2. Taking Notes in Class

Students must be taught effective ways to write down the important information presented by their teachers. In this chapter students are taught a strategy for taking class notes.

Chapter 3. Reading and Taking Notes from Textbooks

Much of the information students must learn in school is contained in their textbooks. Students must be taught effective ways to read their textbooks and take notes on important information. To do so, students must have a textbook reading and notetaking strategy. In this chapter students are taught to use a textbook reading and notetaking strategy called SQ3R.

Chapter 4. Understanding Graphic Aids

Students must be taught how to interpret maps, graphs, diagrams, tables, and charts to increase their understanding of information found in textual materials. In this chapter students are taught how to interpret these graphic aids.

Chapter 5. Remembering Important Information

Learning something is of little value if what is learned cannot be recalled whenever necessary. In this chapter students are taught strategies for retaining the important information and ideas they learn from their teachers and textual materials.

Chapter 6. Preparing for and Taking Tests

Students must demonstrate mastery of information by taking tests given in different formats. Many times students have learned information but lack the test preparation and test-taking skills needed to demonstrate their knowledge. In this chapter students are taught a five-day strategy for preparing for tests. They are also taught how to do well on the following types of tests: multiple-choice, true/false, matching, completion, and essay.

Chapter 7. Solving Math Word Problems

Having a strategy helps students solve math word problems. In this chapter students are taught to use a math word problem solving strategy called SQRQCQ. They then are taught to apply the strategy to different types of math word problems.

Chapter 8. Using the Library

Students must be taught to make appropriate use of the many print and electronic resources found in libraries. In this chapter students are taught strategies for using these resources to search for information.

Chapter 9. Using the Internet

The Internet is a popular tool for locating information. In this chapter students are taught about various services offered on the Internet. Students are also taught strategies to evaluate information found on the Internet.

Chapter 10. Using Reference Sources

Students must be made aware of the many reference sources they can use to achieve success in school. In this chapter students are taught strategies for using both print and electronic forms of the following: dictionary, encyclopedia, thesaurus, almanac, and atlas.

Chapter 11. Writing a Research Paper

Students must be able to do library research and write a research paper. They must be taught to obtain, document, and organize print and electronic information and present it in a clear, written form. In this chapter students are taught a strategic series of steps to follow when writing a research paper.

HOW THIS BOOK IS ORGANIZED

Each chapter is organized as follows:

1. Chapter Objectives
2. Titles of Reproducible Activities
3. Suggestions for Using the Reproducible Activities
4. Reproducible Activities
5. Chapter Mastery Assessment
6. Answers for Chapter Reproducible Activities

HOW TO USE THIS BOOK

1. Use the results from 3S–Gr 4–8 to select the chapters most appropriate for your students.
2. Duplicate the reproducible activities you wish to use.
3. Use Suggestions for Using the Reproducible Activities and your own ideas to provide instruction.
4. Have students complete the Chapter Mastery Assessment at any point you feel they have learned the study skills and strategies presented in a chapter.

TEACHING NOTES

Here are some things to do when using this book:

1. Go beyond the reproducibles to provide your students with additional practice in the use of the strategies. It is additional practice with materials that are directly related to classroom objectives that will enable students to achieve greater success in school.
2. Have the students use a study strategy under your supervision until they have mastered it. Mastery of a strategy means that students are able to recall it as rapidly as they can recall their own

names or phone numbers. Mastery also means the ability to apply the strategy automatically to school tasks. Students have achieved mastery when they can automatically recall and apply a strategy. Until they have achieved this automaticity, there is no mastery.

3. Share the strategies with colleagues who also teach your students, and encourage your colleagues to have the students use the strategies in their classes as well. This will help to ensure that students generalize and maintain their use of the strategies.
4. Although the various study strategies are presented individually in this book, in reality students will need to use a combination of strategies to complete most assignments. For example, students studying for a test should use strategies for remembering information, reading textbooks, and managing time, in addition to test-taking strategies. Use every opportunity to demonstrate or explain to your students how to combine the use of the various strategies presented in this book.
5. Motivate your students to want to use the study strategies taught in this book. We recommend you use the PARS motivation strategy. This strategy has four components: Purpose, Attitude, Results, Success.
    - Purpose. Students are more likely to want to learn a study strategy when they understand how the strategy can help them succeed in school. Be sure to explain how its use can help them acquire more information and get better grades in your class and in their other classes.
    - Attitude. Your attitude is infectious. If you are enthusiastic about a study strategy, your enthusiasm will transfer to your students, who are then likely to model your positive attitude toward the use of the strategy.
    - Results. It is important to give students feedback on how well they are applying a strategy. The feedback needs to be very specific so that students understand what they did correctly and what they did wrong. Students need specific feedback in order to know what to do to improve their use of each strategy.
    - Success. It is important that students experience success in the application of a strategy. Nothing elicits recurrent behavior as well as success.
6. Have students work cooperatively in pairs or small groups to practice applying the strategies to class assignments. Students can take turns demonstrating how a strategy is used or providing feedback on the effectiveness of its use.

ACKNOWLEDGMENTS

We express our appreciation to our colleagues at the University of Miami and Florida International University who graciously gave their time to review the activities in this book. Their reactions and recommendations were of great assistance to us. We also wish to acknowledge our university students, most of whom are classroom teachers. Feedback from their trial use of the activities in their classrooms allowed us to make important improvements.

About the Authors

Teaching Study Skills and Strategies in Grades 4–8 is the equal and shared work of the following authors:

Charles T. Mangrum II is professor of special education and reading at the University of Miami, Coral Gables, Florida. He graduated from Northern Michigan University and taught elementary and secondary school before entering graduate school. He earned a Ed.D. from Indiana University in 1968. Since 1968 he has been on the faculty at the University of Miami, where he trains teachers who teach students with reading and learning disabilities. Dr. Mangrum is the author of many books, instructional programs, and articles on topics related to reading and study skills.

Patricia Iannuzzi is University Librarian and Head of the Reference Department at Florida International University Libraries. She graduated from Yale University and earned an M.S. in Library and Information Science at Simmons College in 1980. Ms. Iannuzzi has worked in libraries at Tufts University, Yale University, and the University of California at Berkeley. Since 1990 she has been on the library faculty at Florida International University, where she manages reference services, develops information literacy curricula, and teaches information literacy skills in subjects across the curriculum.

Stephen S. Strichart is professor of special education and learning disabilities at Florida International University, Miami, Florida. He graduated from City College of New York and taught children with various types of disabilities before entering graduate school. Dr. Strichart earned a Ph.D. from Yeshiva University in 1972. Since 1975 he has been on the faculty at Florida International University, where he trains teachers and psychologists to work with exceptional students. Dr. Strichart is the author of many books and articles on topics related to special education and study skills.

CHAPTER ONE

Using Study Time, Habits, Space

CHAPTER OBJECTIVES

1. **Teach students a strategy for using time effectively.**
2. **Teach students to evaluate and improve their study habits.**
3. **Teach students to evaluate and improve their study place.**

TITLES OF REPRODUCIBLE ACTIVITIES

1-1 A Strategy for Using Time Effectively
1-2 Using a Term Calendar
1-3 Term Calendar
1-4 Using a Weekly Planner
1-5 Weekly Planner
1-6 Using a Daily Organizer
1-7 Daily Organizer
1-8 Study Habits Checklist
1-9 Improving Your Study Habits
1-10 Study Place Checklist
1-11 Improving Your Study Place
1-12 Chapter One Mastery Assessment

SUGGESTIONS FOR USING THE REPRODUCIBLE ACTIVITIES

1-1 A Strategy for Using Time Effectively

Lead students in a discussion of the importance of using time effectively. Tell them successful students schedule and manage time to be able to complete all their schoolwork and responsibilities, yet still have some time for fun. Discuss each of the three components of the strategy, and have students describe each in writing.

1-2 Using a Term Calendar

1-3 Term Calendar

Discuss the purposes of a term calendar. Review the four steps students should follow to prepare a term calendar. Have students list on 1-2 their school assignments, school activities, and out-of-school activities for the term. Tell students to include dates. Distribute copies of 1-3. Have students record information from 1-2 on 1-3. Tell students they can record special notes about the things they have to do in the section headed "Notes" at the bottom of the term calendar. Explain how to use an asterisk (*) to mark the first note, a double asterisk (**) for the second note, and so on.

1-4 Using a Weekly Planner
1-5 Weekly Planner

Discuss the purposes of a weekly planner. Review the three steps for preparing a weekly planner. Have students complete the items in 1-4 for the coming week. Distribute copies of 1-5. Have students record information from 1-4 on 1-5. Repeat this procedure for each week.

1-6 Using a Daily Organizer
1-7 Daily Organizer

Discuss the purposes of a daily organizer. Review the five steps for preparing a daily organizer. Have students complete the items in 1-6 for the next day. Distribute copies of 1-7. Have students record information from 1-6 on 1-7. Remind students to complete a daily organizer each evening.

1-8 Study Habits Checklist

Lead students in a discussion of the importance of good study habits. Then have students complete 1-8.

1-9 Improving Your Study Habits

Have students write any study habits for which they checked "No" on 1-8. For each study habit included, have them write a suggestion for improving it. Have students share their suggestions with the class.

1-10 Study Place Checklist

Discuss with students the importance of having a good place to study. Then have students complete 1-10.

1-11 Improving Your Study Place

Have students write any study place feature for which they checked "No" on 1-10. For each study place feature included, have them write a suggestion for improving it. Have students share their suggestions with the class.

1-12 Chapter One Mastery Assessment

Have students complete this assessment at any point you feel they have learned about effective use of time, study habits, and study space. Review the results of the assessment with the students. Recycle students through activities as needed.

A Strategy for Using Time Effectively 1-1

Do you ever wonder how some students seem to get their work done and still have lots of time to do other things? These students schedule their time so they can get everything done they want to do. These students have an effective strategy for using time. You must also have an effective strategy for using your time. This means you must do the following:

1. Prepare a **Term Calendar** that shows all your major school and out-of-school activities and assignments for a term. Your term calendar should be prepared at the beginning of each term. As the term goes on, you will continually add new items to the calendar.
2. Prepare a **Weekly Planner** that shows your school and out-of-school activities and assignments due for the upcoming week. Your weekly planner should be prepared over the weekend before each week begins.
3. Prepare a **Daily Organizer** to show what you must do each day and when you plan to do it. This is your daily plan and should be prepared each night for the next day.

Describe the three steps in the strategy for effectively using time.

1.

2.

3.

Using a Term Calendar **1-2**

To do all the things you want to do each term, you need to schedule your time. A term calendar will remind you when you need to start and finish important school and out-of-school activities. It will help you plan your time so you do not schedule more things than you can possibly do.

A **Term Calendar** helps you to organize your school and out-of-school activities. Here is how you use it:

1. Ask each of your teachers for a list of assignments and dates and place them on your term calendar. Be sure to enter all the regular, midterm, and final examination dates as well as the dates that papers and projects are due.
2. Get a list of the school activities for the current term. Enter the activities you plan to be part of on your term calendar.
3. Make a list of the out-of-school activities in which you plan to be involved. These include such things as attending sporting events, going to club meetings, and going on family trips. Enter each on your term calendar.
4. Record any special notes about the things you have to do in the section headed "NOTES" at the bottom of the term calendar. Use an * for the first note, ** for the second note, and so on.

Now list the school assignments you know you will have this term. Also provide their dates.

Then list the school activities you know you will be involved with this term. Also provide their dates.

Next list the out-of-school activities you know you will be involved with this term. Also provide their dates.

Finally, list any special notes.

Use these lists to complete the term calendar provided to you by your teacher.

Term Calendar

1-3

NAME ______________________ DATES COVERED ______________________

Monday	Tuesday	Wednesday	Thursday	Friday

NOTES:

Using a Weekly Planner **1-4**

During each weekend you need to spend some time preparing your plan for the upcoming week. A weekly planner will help you do this. The weekly planner is used to show in detail what you are planning to do during that week. Here is how to prepare your weekly planner:

1. Review your term calendar to see what you planned to do during the week. Enter this information into your weekly planner.
2. Review notes from your classes to see what else needs to be added to your weekly planner.
3. Think about the out-of-school activities you need to do during the upcoming week. Add them to your weekly planner.

Now list items from your term calendar that you need to record in your weekly planner.

Next list items from your notes that need to be recorded in your weekly planner.

Then list out-of-school activities you need to do.

Finally, list any special notes.

Use these lists to complete the weekly planner provided to you by your teacher.

Weekly Planner **1-5**

NAME ______________________ WEEK OF ______________

	MONDAY	TUESDAY	WEDNESDAY	THURSDAY	FRIDAY	SATURDAY	SUNDAY
9:00							
10:00							
11:00							
12:00							
1:00							
2:00							
3:00							
4:00							
5:00							
EVENING							

NOTES:

Using a Daily Organizer **1-6**

Each evening before a school day, you need to prepare a daily organizer. The daily organizer shows how you will use your time each day. It helps you arrange your time so you get everything done you want to do. It keeps you from wasting time. Here is how to prepare your daily organizer.

1. Review your weekly planner to see what you need to do tomorrow.
2. Review your class notes to see what else you need to add.
3. Review your daily organizer for today to determine what you did not get done. Add these things to your daily organizer for tomorrow.
4. For each thing you need to do tomorrow, decide how much time you need to do it.
5. Decide when you will do each thing. Write the thing you need to do in the appropriate time period in your daily organizer.

Now list the things from your weekly planner that you need to do tomorrow. Next to each, tell how much time you need to do it.

Then list things from your class notes you know you need to do tomorrow. Tell how much time you will need to do each thing.

Next list things you did not finish today and that you will need to do tomorrow. Tell how much time you will need to do each thing.

Finally, list any special notes.

Use your list to complete the daily organizer provided by your teacher.

Daily Organizer **1-7**

NAME ______________________ DAY/DATE ______________________

7:00 ______________________

8:00 ______________________

9:00 ______________________

10:00 ______________________

11:00 ______________________

12:00 ______________________

1:00 ______________________

2:00 ______________________

3:00 ______________________

4:00 ______________________

5:00 ______________________

6:00 ______________________

7:00 ______________________

8:00 ______________________

NOTES:

Study Habits Checklist **1-8**

You need good study habits to get good grades. Good grades just don't happen—they come as a result of good study habits. Use the following checklist to see how good your study habits are. Read each statement describing a study habit. For each check (√) "Yes" or "No."

My Study Habits	*Yes*	*No*
I have a planned study time.		
I tell my friends not to call me during my study time.		
I start working on time.		
I review my notes before beginning an assignment.		
I begin with the hardest assignment.		
I finish one assignment before going on to another.		
I take short breaks when I feel tired.		
I avoid daydreaming.		
I have a "study buddy" I can contact when I get stuck.		
I write down questions I will need to ask my teacher.		
I keep working on long-term assignments.		

Improving Your Study Habits **1-9**

List the study habits you need to improve in order to get better grades. Include any study habit for which you checked "No" when completing the Study Habits Checklist on 1-8. Write something you can do to improve this study habit.

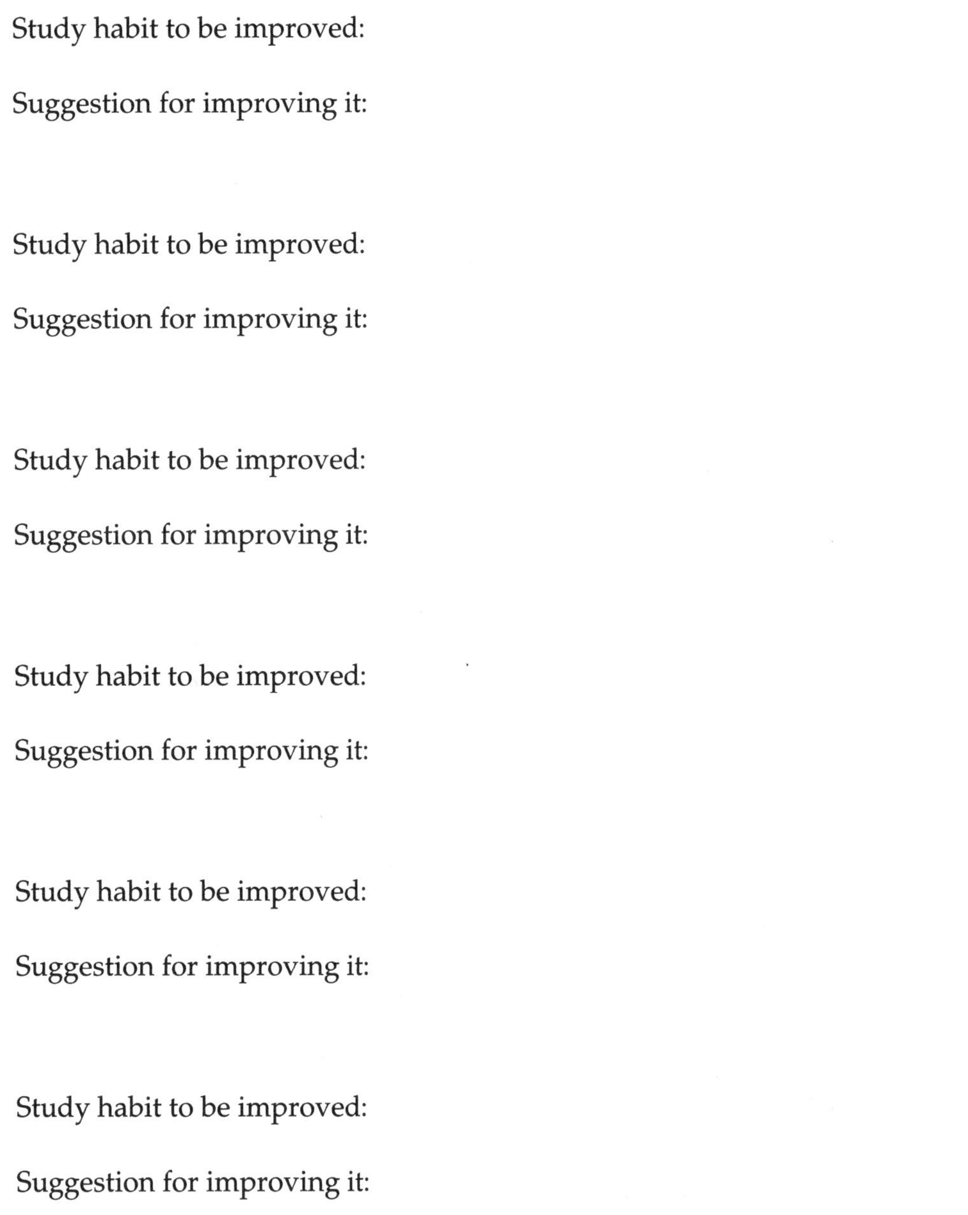

Study habit to be improved:

Suggestion for improving it:

Study habit to be improved:

Suggestion for improving it:

Study habit to be improved:

Suggestion for improving it:

Study habit to be improved:

Suggestion for improving it:

Study habit to be improved:

Suggestion for improving it:

Study habit to be improved:

Suggestion for improving it:

Study Place Checklist

1-10

You need a good study place at home. How you arrange your study place has a lot to do with how well you will study and learn. If your study place is a noisy, busy place full of things that take your attention away from your work, you will not learn much. If there is a telephone, radio, stereo, or television nearby, the temptation to use them may be too much. Thinking about people to call, songs to listen to, or programs to watch takes times away from studying. Time away from studying lowers your grades.

Use the following checklist to see how good your study place is. Read each statement. For each check (√) "Yes" or "No."

My Study Place	*Yes*	*No*
It is quiet.		
There are no things to look at that take my attention away from my work.		
There is good light.		
The temperature is comfortable.		
There is a comfortable chair.		
It contains all the work materials I need.		
It contains all the reference sources I need.		
It contains a desk or table large enough to work at comfortably.		
It contains enough storage space.		
I can use this study place whenever I need it.		

Improving Your Study Place **1-11**

List the features that need to be improved in your study place. Include any feature for which you checked "No" when completing the Study Place Checklist on 1-10. For each one included, write something you can do to improve this feature of your study place.

Feature that needs to be improved:

Suggestion for improving it:

Feature that needs to be improved:

Suggestion for improving it:

Feature that needs to be improved:

Suggestion for improving it:

Feature that needs to be improved:

Suggestion for improving it:

Feature that needs to be improved:

Suggestion for improving it:

Feature that needs to be improved:

Suggestion for improving it:

Chapter One Mastery Assessment 1-12

Directions Show what you have learned about study times, habits, and space by writing an answer for each of the following:

1. Why do you need to prepare a term calendar?

2. Weekly planner?

3. Daily organizer?

4. How can using the Study Habits Checklist help you become a better student?

5. How can using the Study Place Checklist help you become a better student?

ANSWERS FOR CHAPTER ONE REPRODUCIBLE ACTIVITIES

1-1 1. Prepare a term calendar showing major things to do both in and out of school for the term. 2. Prepare a weekly calendar showing in- and out-of-school activities for the upcoming week. 3. Prepare a daily organizer to show what must be done tomorrow.

1-2 Answers will vary.

1-3 Entries will vary according to the information recorded on 1-2.

1-4 Answer will vary.

1-5 Entries will vary according to the information recorded on 1-4.

1-6 Answers will vary.

1-7 Entries will vary according to the information recorded on 1-6.

1-8 Answers will vary.

1-9 Entries will vary according to the information recorded on 1-8.

1-10 Answers will vary.

1-11 Entries will vary according to the information recorded on 1-10.

1-12 1. To have a long-range plan for organizing in-school and out-of-school activities for the term. 2. To prepare for the requirements of the upcoming week. 3. To show what you must do each day and when you expect to do it. 4. By identifying study habits that need to be improved. 5. By identifying study place features that need to be improved.

CHAPTER TWO

Taking Notes in Class

CHAPTER OBJECTIVES

1. **Teach students the three stages of notetaking.**
2. **Teach students to take notes.**

TITLES OF REPRODUCIBLE ACTIVITIES

2-1 The First Two Stages of Notetaking
2-2 Signal Words
2-3 Signal Statements
2-4 Writing Shorter Sentences or Phrases
2-5 Abbreviating Words
2-6 Abbreviating Statements
2-7 Two-Column Notetaking
2-8 Rough Notes
2-9 The Third Stage of Notetaking
2-10 Revised Notes
2-11 Graphic Organizer for Revised Notes
2-12 Chapter Two Mastery Assessment

SUGGESTIONS FOR USING THE REPRODUCIBLE ACTIVITIES

2-1 The First Two Stages of Notetaking

Introduce the first two of three stages of the notetaking strategy (the third stage is presented in Activity 2-9). The "Get Ready" stage contains statements describing what students should do to prepare to take notes in class. The "Take Notes" stage contains statements describing what students should do while taking notes. Elaborate on each statement. Encourage students to write key ideas in the space provided after each statement.

2-2 Signal Words

Introduce the signal words *first, second, next, finally,* and *several.* Tell students that these words signal that what follows is important. Have students locate these signal words in "Losing Your Hair." Tell students that teachers use the same words as signals when they speak or lecture. Have students share other signal words they have heard teachers use.

2-3 Signal Statements

Introduce statements teachers use to signal important information. Review the signal statements provided as examples. Have students add others. Then have students identify signal statements in "The Roman Army."

2-4 Writing Shorter Sentences or Phrases

Tell students that speakers usually talk faster than writers write. To capture the important points in a lecture, students should write in short sentences or phrases rather than long sentences. Have students rewrite the long sentences into shorter sentences or phrases.

2-5 Abbreviating Words

Tell students that a good way to increase notetaking speed is by abbreviating words whenever possible. Use the examples to demonstrate how words can be abbreviated. Then have the students complete the activity on their own.

2-6 Abbreviating Statements

Tell students they can sometimes abbreviate entire statements. Use the examples to demonstrate how this is done. Then have students complete the activity using standard abbreviations or ones they create.

2-7 Two-Column Notetaking

Introduce the two-column notetaking format. Point out the identifying information that students should include at the top of each notetaking page. **Rough Notes** is where students record notes while listening to a teacher. **Don't Understand** is where they write anything they do not understand. **New Vocabulary** is where they write new words whose meaning they will have to learn.

2-8 Rough Notes

Guide students through an examination of the three sections of the note-taking format shown on this page. Call attention to the written notes, the questions asked, and the unknown words listed.

2-9 The Third Stage of Notetaking

Tell students that "After Taking Notes" is the third stage of the three stage notetaking strategy. During this stage, students revise their rough notes. Elaborate on each statement. Encourage students to write key ideas in the space provided after each statement.

2-10 Revised Notes

Use as an example of how notes were rewritten to revise them. Call attention to the **boldface type**, which shows how some text was changed and other text moved to provide better organization.

2-11 Graphic Organizer for Revised Notes

Tell students that another way to show their revised notes is by creating a graphic organizer. Use this activity to show students a graphic organizer for the revised notes in 2-10.

2-12 Chapter Two Mastery Assessment

Have students complete this assessment at any point you believe they have learned the notetaking skills presented in this chapter. Review the results of the assessment with the students. Provide additional instruction as necessary.

The First Two Stages of Notetaking **2-1**

Listen as your teacher tells you about the first two stages of a three-stage strategy for taking notes in class. After each numbered statement, write any key ideas you want to remember.

GET READY

1. Have notetaking materials ready.

2. Review notes.

3. Do all assigned reading.

4. Identify your purpose(s) for listening.

TAKE NOTES

1. Listen for your purpose(s).

2. Use short sentences, phrases, and abbreviations.

3. Skip lines between new ideas.

4. Copy information from the chalkboard.

5. Note things you do not understand.

6. Note words whose meaning you do not know.

Signal Words **2-2**

During a lecture your teacher often will use words that tell you something is very important to write down. These words are called *signal words*. If you listen for signal words, you will be more likely to write down important information.

Here are some signal words used by teachers that tell you what they are about to say is important to write down. Get to know these signal words.

first second finally next several

Read the following selection to see how these signal words call your attention to important information. Underline each of these signal words as you read the selection.

Losing Your Hair

As people get older they typically lose some of their hair. Men usually lose their hair at an earlier age than women. However, there are many bald women just as there are bald men. People don't like to lose their hair because they think it makes them look older. There are several things that can be done to stop the loss of hair. The first thing most people try is to take better care of their hair by regular shampooing. There are many different types of shampoos available, many of which promise to stop the loss of hair. The second remedy is to massage the scalp regularly with a stiff brush or with one's fingers. When this doesn't work, the next thing people usually try is a vitamin therapy. There are many different vitamins that are thought to encourage hair growth.

Finally, when all else fails, people go out and buy a wig or toupee. Both are used to cover part or all of the scalp. As you can see, it is natural to lose hair, but there are things you can do to keep that "young look."

Write the signal words you learned about in this activity in the order they appeared in this selection.

Signal Statements **2-3**

Sometimes teachers use statements instead of single words to signal important information. Teachers may use statements such as:

"Here is something you should know."
"I wouldn't forget this point if I were you."
"Remember this."
"This is particularly important."
"There are five things you have to know."

1. Think of other statements teachers use to signal important information. Write them here.

Read the following selection and underline any statements that signal important information.

The Roman Army

The expansion of Rome was made possible in part by the courage and skill of its soldiers. Be sure to remember that the Roman army became a match for any army in the Western world. The Roman army was made up mostly of foot soldiers. In early times, the soldiers were organized into groups of 8,000 called phalanxes. Make sure that you know that a phalanx was a group of soldiers massed together with shields joined and spears overlapping. Later the army replaced phalanxes with legions. A legion was made up of 3,600 men. Write in your notes that the legion was much more effective in battle than a phalanx. Roman soldiers were tough, loyal, practical men. The major thing to know is that they could handle just about any task from repairing weapons to sewing their own clothes. They had to obey rules or face a very severe punishment. The most important point is that because of its great army, Rome took over all of Italy. I am going to expect you to know that when the Roman army began to weaken, Rome began to lose its control of Italy.

2. Write the signal statements you found in this selection.

Writing Shorter Sentences or Phrases **2-4**

When you take notes, you should use phrases or short sentences as often as possible. For example, instead of writing the long sentence, "As air cools it loses its ability to hold water vapor," you could write, "Cool air can't hold water vapor."

For each sentence below, rewrite the sentence in a shorter form or as a phrase.

1. As we have noted, the Constitution gives to each branch of the government its own distinctive field of governmental authority: legislative, executive, and judicial.

2. The weight at which you look and feel most comfortable is your "ideal" weight or the healthiest weight for your body.

3. Any water used for drinking purposes not only must be free of salt but also should be free of foreign matter.

4. The common cold is really a group of symptoms and signs caused by a variety of viruses.

5. Each of the American colonies was born out of a particular set of circumstances, and so each had its own character.

Abbreviating Words **2-5**

When taking notes, it is important to write quickly. A good way to increase your notetaking speed is to use abbreviations. An abbreviation is a short way of writing something. Here are some words and the abbreviations that can be used to write these words in a short way:

Words	*Abbreviations*	*Words*	*Abbreviations*
psychology	psy	medicine	med
English	Eng	diameter	dia
month	mo	year	yr
vocabulary	vocab	Florida	Fl

Here are some common words. For each word, write an abbreviation. You can make up any abbreviation as long as you are able to recognize the word from your abbreviation.

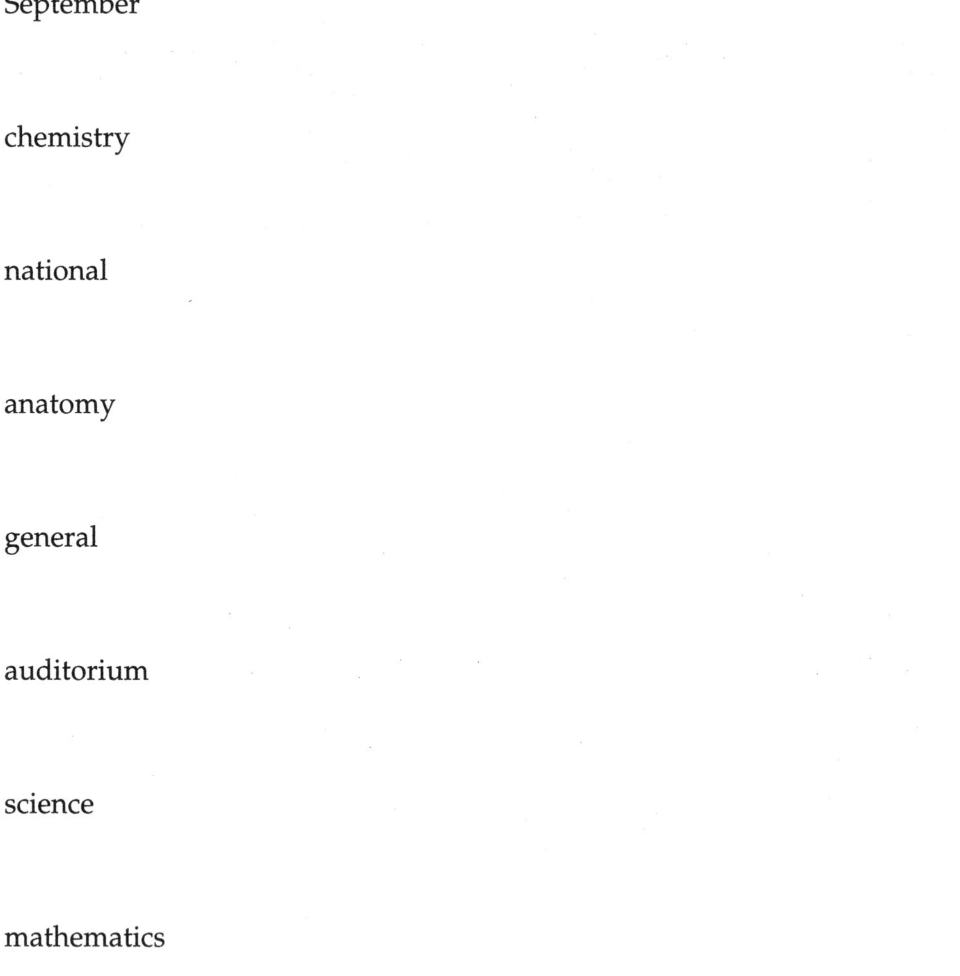

September

chemistry

national

anatomy

general

auditorium

science

mathematics

Abbreviating Statements **2-6**

Sometimes you can write entire statements with abbreviations. For example, you can abbreviate "grade point average" as "gpa" or "home computer" as "ho comp." You can also abbreviate the names of organizations or titles. For example, the Federal Bureau of Investigation is commonly known as the FBI. Likewise, the chief executive officer of a company is commonly known as the CEO.

Create an abbreviation that will help you recall each of the following:

1. United States of America
2. Internal Revenue Service
3. National Aeronautics and Space Administration
4. Central Intelligence Agency
5. North Atlantic Treaty Organization
6. United States Air Force
7. school principal
8. biology textbook
9. homework
10. longitude and latitude

Two-Column Notetaking

2-7

Class ________________ Period ________________ Date ________________ Page ____

Rough Notes	Don't Understand

New Vocabulary

Rough Notes

2-8

Class U.S. History Period 3 Date 10/14/91 Page 1

Rough Notes	Don't Understand
Mining gold means taking it out of ground.	
Gold is valuable—costs lot. Soft. Lasts forever. Not much of it.	
Uses of gold—watches and rings coins and gold bars jewelry expensive jewelry	How is gold used in teeth?
Gold is found all over world—For example US Russia Australia	
3 ways to mine gold	
1. placer mining—panning. 49ers used pan to scoop gold from a stream using sand. 49ers went to California & found gold at Sutter's Mill in 1849. Bought grub—food. Got a grubstake.	Is there gold in California now? Are there miners now?
2. Vein mining. ½ the gold gotten this way. Looked for mother lode.	
3. Processing other metals. Get gold as by-product. Get more than placer mining—but not as much as vein mining.	

New Vocabulary:
- by-product
- grubstake
- vein

The Third Stage of Notetaking

2-9

Listen as your teacher tells you about the third stage of a three-stage strategy for taking notes in class. After each numbered statement, write any key ideas you want to remember.

After taking notes:

1. Add important information left out of rough notes.

2. Answer any questions in the "Don't Understand" column.

3. Complete any blanks in the rough notes.

4. Write definitions for each unknown word.

Class U.S. History Period 3 Date 10/14/91 Page 1

Rough Notes	Don't Understand
Mining gold means taking it out of ground.	
Gold is valuable—costs lot. Soft. Lasts forever. Not much of it.	
The 49ers went to California & found gold at Sutter's Mill in 1849. **They bought grub—food. Got a grubstake.**	Is there gold in California now? Are there miners there? **There are some commercial gold mines. Also, some independent miners are still prospecting for gold.**
Uses of gold—watches, rings / coins, bars / jewelry; **industry** / **medicine** / expensive jewelry	How is gold used in teeth? **Gold is used to fill cavities in teeth and sometimes to make new teeth.**
Gold is found all over the world—For example U.S. Russia Australia	
3 ways to mine gold 1. placer mining—panning. 49ers used pan to scoop gold from a stream using sand. 2. Vein mining. ½ the gold gotten this way. **Miners find veins of gold in the mountains. Break off pieces of rock and follow vein to find all the gold.** Looked for mother lode. 3. Processing other metals. Get gold as a by-product. Get more than placer mining—but not as much as vein mining.	

New Vocabulary

by-product	**Something produced in the making of something else.**
grubstake	**Money or supplies advanced to a prospector against future profits.**
vein	**Like a vein in the body but its ore and its found in rock.**

Graphic Organizer for Revised Notes

2-11

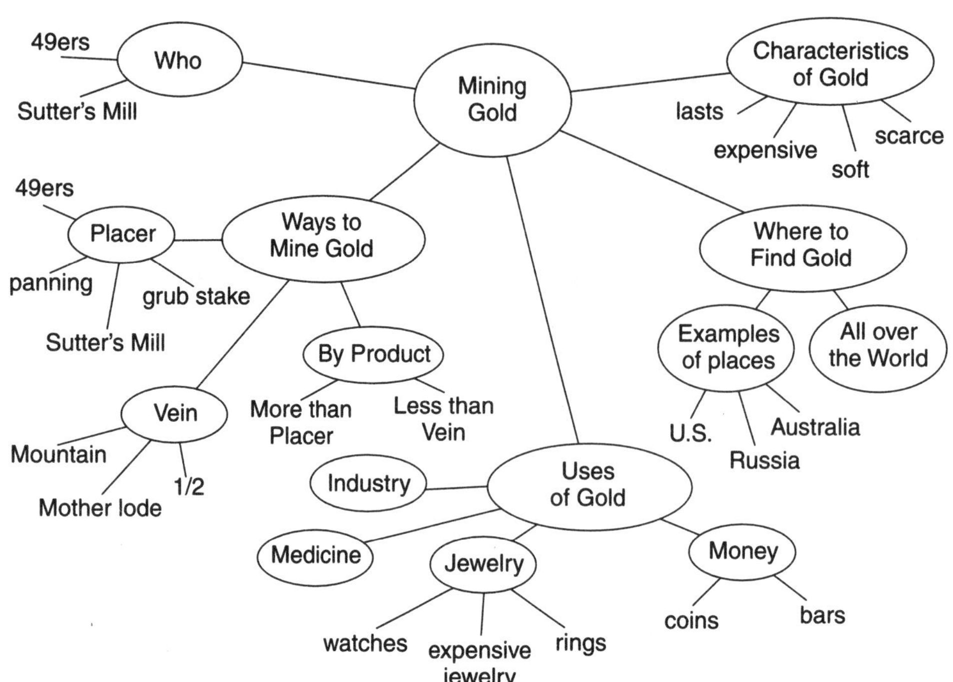

Chapter Two Mastery Assessment

Directions Show what you have learned about taking notes in class by completing the following. First, write the name of each stage in the notetaking strategy. Next, list the things to do for each stage.

Stage 1 ____________________

1. ____________________
2. ____________________
3. ____________________
4. ____________________

Stage 2 ____________________

1. ____________________
2. ____________________
3. ____________________
4. ____________________
5. ____________________
6. ____________________

Stage 3 ____________________

1. ____________________
2. ____________________
3. ____________________
4. ____________________

ANSWERS FOR CHAPTER TWO REPRODUCIBLE ACTIVITIES

2-1 Students' key ideas will vary.
2-2 Several, first, second, next, finally.
2-3 1. Answers will vary. 2. Be sure to remember; Make sure that you know; Write in your notes; The major thing to know; The most important point; I am going to expect you to know.
2-4 Answers will vary.
2-5 Answers will vary.
2-6 1. USA. 2. IRS. 3. NASA. 4. CIA. 5. NATO. 6. USAF. 7–10. Answers will vary.
2-7 No writing required.
2-8 No writing required.
2-9 Students' key ideas will vary.
2-10 No writing required.
2-11 No writing required.
2-12 **Get Ready:** 1. Have notetaking materials ready. 2. Review your notes. 3. Do all assigned reading. 4. Identify your purpose(s) for listening.
Take Notes: 1. Listen for your purpose(s). 2. Use short sentences, phrases, and abbreviations. 3. Skip lines between new ideas. 4. Copy information from the chalkboard. 5. Note things you do not understand. 6. Note words whose meaning you do not know.
After Taking Notes: 1. Add important information left out of rough notes. 2. Answer any questions in the "Don't Understand" column. 3. Complete any blanks in the rough notes. 4. Write definitions for each unknown word.

CHAPTER THREE

Reading and Taking Notes from Textbooks

CHAPTER OBJECTIVES

1. **Teach students to use the SQ3R textbook reading and notetaking strategy.**
2. **Teach students to apply SQ3R to textbook reading assignments.**

TITLES OF REPRODUCIBLE ACTIVITIES

3-1 Learning about SQ3R
3-2 Reading Assignment: "A Visit to Ancient Rome"
3-3 Textbook Notes for "A Visit to Ancient Rome"
3-4 Reading Assignment: "Political Parties"
3-5 Textbook Notes for "Political Parties"
3-6 Reading Assignment: "What Europeans Found"
3-7 Textbook Notes for "What Europeans Found"
3-8 Chapter Three Mastery Assessment

SUGGESTIONS FOR USING THE REPRODUCIBLE ACTIVITIES

3-1 Learning about SQ3R

Tell students they will be learning how to use a strategy for reading and taking notes from assignments in textbooks. Use this activity to help students associate SQ3R with the words *Survey, Question, Read, Recite,* and *Review*. Use the directions following each word to help students understand what they are to do for each step in the strategy. They will be using this strategy with several reading assignments throughout this chapter.

3-2 Textbook Assignment: "A Visit to Ancient Rome"
3-3 Textbook Notes for "A Visit to Ancient Rome"

Have students survey "A Visit to Ancient Rome" on 3-2. Next have students change the title and headings into questions and write the questions on 3-3. Remind students that they can write more than one question for a title or heading. Finally, have students read to answer the questions and write their answers on 3-3. Sample answers are provided at the end of the chapter.

3-4 Textbook Assignment: "Political Parties"
3-5 Textbook Notes for "Political Parties"

Have students write the words that go with SQRRR. Then have students survey "Political Parties" on 3-4. Next have students change the title and headings into questions and write the questions on 3-5. Remind students that they can write more than one question for a title or heading. Finally, have students read to answer the questions and write their answers on 3-5. Sample answers are provided at the end of the chapter.

3-6 Textbook Assignment: "What Europeans Found"
3-7 Textbook Notes for "What Europeans Found"

Have students survey "What Europeans Found" on 3-6. Next have students change the title and headings into questions and write the questions on 3-7. Remind students that they can write more than one question for a title or heading. Finally have students read to answer the questions and write their answers on 3-7. Sample answers are provided at the end of the chapter.

3-8 Chapter Three Mastery Assessment

Have students complete this assessment at any point you believe they have learned to use SQ3R. Review the results of the assessment with the students. Provide additional instruction as necessary.

Learning about SQ3R

3-1

1. Survey

- Read the **title** and think about what it means.
- Read the **introduction,** which is usually found in the first paragraph or two.
- Read the **headings** to learn what the selection is about.
- Examine all the **visuals** and read their **captions.**
- Read the **conclusion,** which is usually found in the last paragraph or two.

2. Question

- Change the **title** into one or more questions. Use these key words to form your questions: ***who, what, where, when, why, how.***
- Change each **heading** into one or more questions. Use these key words to form your questions: ***who, what, where, when, why, how.***
- **Write** the questions.

3. Read

- **Read** to **answer** the **questions.**
- **Change questions,** as necessary, to answer the questions the author is addressing.
- **Write answers** to questions to form textbook notes.

4. Recite

Immediately following the reading assignment, do the following for each question:

- Read the question and its answer **aloud.**
- Read the question **aloud,** then look away and say the answer **aloud.**
- Read the question **aloud,** then with eyes closed say the answer **aloud.**
- Repeat these steps three times.

5. Review

Review by doing the same things you did for the **recite** step. Do this once each day for the next three days. Review for more than three days if you need to.

A VISIT TO ANCIENT ROME

What do you think living in Rome was like a thousand or more years ago? It was quite exciting for the times because Rome was the cultural center of the known world. By taking a visit to ancient Rome, you will obtain a feeling for this marvelous city.

Roman Dress

The first thing a traveler to ancient Rome would see would be some male citizens going about their daily business dressed in long, woolen shirts called tunics. Those men who were involved in more formal routines would be wearing undyed wool togas over their tunics. In most weather all Romans wore strap sandals. The ladies of the city dressed in long stolas, tunics belted at the waist, worn over an inner tunic. They might wear a rectangular cloak if the weather was cold. Roman women often carried parasols and fans in hot weather. All the citizens dressed as comfortably as they could.

Forms of Entertainment

As he toured the city, the newcomer might wonder what forms of entertainment amused the citizens. He would probably hear shouts and cheers coming from an area where spectators were enjoying a circus, a play, or gladiatorial combat. These events took place often and lasted from sunrise to sundown. Admission was free so anyone who chose to could attend.

Another popular leisure time activity in ancient Rome was public bathing. Bathing establishments were quite elaborate. One would find games, lectures, and musical performances presented there. There were areas where people could lounge and gossip if they were not enjoying the baths. At the center of everything were the baths themselves, a cold bath, a warm bath, and a steam bath which bathers passed through in order. The baths were actually a large complex of business and entertainment areas.

Limitations of the City

The tourist would be impressed with the Roman's love of grandeur as evidence by the beauty of baths, but if he walked around the city long enough, he would become aware of the limitations it had. It would soon be obvious that as a visitor he would have to ask directions in order to get around. Most of the residential streets did not have names and the houses did not have numbers. There were few sidewalks and the streets were narrow and crowded. The tourist would have to be alert when he strolled down a residential street because at that time people disposed of their trash the easiest way, by throwing it out the window! Thus, walking around Rome was not only confusing, it was also dangerous.

Rome at Night

Anyone visiting Rome would be well advised to do his sightseeing during the day because a walk through Rome at night was a dangerous adventure. There were no street lights to illuminate the heavy traffic that clogged the streets. During the day law prohibited chariots and tradesmen's carts from filling the streets of the city, so there was a great deal of traffic at night. There was also a lot of crime in the dark, crowded streets. Smart Romans stayed at home after sunset.

Hazards of Travel

When the visitor to Rome decided to leave, he would have to choose his route home carefully. Travel outside the city was dangerous and difficult. Wealthy people traveled by carriage, usually accompanied by their household slaves and servants. Travelers would not stop at the inns and hotels along the way because they were apt to be dirty. They also tended to be the hangouts of robbers. Instead the Roman traveler would sleep in his carriage or in a tent put up by the side of the road. If the traveler was fortunate and had a friend who lived along the route, he could stay with him. There was an elaborate social system of *hospitium* or "guest friendship" that was similar to membership in a lodge. People were obligated to give those who were their friends protection and hospitality while they were on the road. Romans had to plan their journey well if they were to arrive at their destination safely.

You can see that living in the ancient city of Rome was both adventurous and dangerous. Life was very different from what we experience in the twentieth century. Dress, entertainment, travel, and conditions of living are much better today.

Textbook Notes for "A Visit to Ancient Rome"

1. **Title:** A Visit to Ancient Rome

   Question

   Answer

2. **Heading:** Roman Dress

   Q

   A

3. **Heading:** Forms of Entertainment

   Q

   A

4. **Heading:** Limitations of the City

   Q

   A

5. **Heading:** Rome at Night

   Q

   A

6. **Heading:** Hazards of Travel

   Q

   A

Reading Assignment: "Political Parties" 3-4

Write the words that go with the letters. Follow this strategy as you read part of a textbook chapter.

S

Q

R

R

R

POLITICAL PARTIES

Political parties propose programs that concern voters. Voters hold public officials accountable. Unless a party makes its program work, voters may vote for the other party in the next election. Thus, the parties provide a way for people to express their support for, or opposition to, the government.

Political Parties and Candidates

One of the most important goals of either the Democratic Party or the Republican Party is to win elections. Each party nominates candidates for public office. The party needs workers and money to get its candidates elected. Therefore, the party must constantly look for workers to help candidates, and raise money to support candidates.

Political parties buy advertising time on television, and advertising space in newspapers. They organize public meetings where candidates can speak. They send workers to homes, shopping centers, factories, and other places to get people to register and to vote. Parties pass out campaign pamphlets and urge people to vote for their candidates. On election day, party workers telephone people registered with their party to remind them to vote. They drive voters to the polls. They offer baby sitting services. It would be very difficult, if not impossible, for a candidate to win an election without party support.

Political Parties in Congress

The Constitution states that each house of Congress may set up its own rules of operation and select its own leaders. In practice, it is the majority party in each house that selects the leaders and decides what the rules will be. Usually the same party has a majority in both houses. Sometimes, however, one party has a majority in the Senate and another has a majority in the House of Representatives.

At the beginning of a new Congress, the members of each party in each house hold a party caucus. At a caucus, each party elects its leader and assigns its members to various committees. The majority and minority leaders are their party's floor leaders and key planners. They try to influence party members to vote on the important bills as the party recommends. When 75 percent of the party's legislators vote the same way, it is considered a party vote.

The majority party in Congress usually has enough support from its members to pass bills. When it does not have this support, the leaders of the majority party may work with leaders of the minority party to get help to pass bills.

One of the advantages of a two-party system is that the two parties will debate issues and work out compromises. Most compromises are made when the majority party needs the minority party's help to pass a bill. At such times, the minority party can have influence over what the bill will contain.

Political Parties and State Legislatures

The Democratic and Republican parties are represented in state legislatures too. The power and influence of the parties in the state legislatures are similar to their power and influence in Congress. Party caucuses elect leaders and assign members to various committees. The majority party elects the leaders in each house. The leaders of each party try to persuade their members to support the bills their party proposes.

The President as a Party Member

You learned in an earlier chapter that Presidents are legislators as well as leaders of their parties. The President, the President's advisers, and the leaders of the President's party in Congress often work together to develop bills.

There are times when the President's views on issues are different from the views of party members in Congress. When this happens they try to compromise, but at times they fail to reach agreement. Members of Congress, for example, may want a large tax cut. The President may feel that taxes should not be reduced. As a result, the President may veto a tax bill that some of his own party members helped to pass.

The President uses the position as party leader and the power to make appointments to reward party members who support presidential programs in Congress. The President may ask these members to suggest people to be appointed as judges, cabinet members, and ambassadors. The President also rewards loyal party members by campaigning for them—making personal appearances and issuing statements of support for them.

As you can see, political parties are an important part of our government system. They provide a way for people with common beliefs to work together to do the important business of government. They also help insure that important issues are debated. Each political party polices the actions of the other party to ensure fairness in government.

Textbook Notes for "Political Parties" 3-5

1. **Title:** Political Parties

   Question

   Answer

2. **Heading:** Political Parties and Candidates

   Q

   A

3. **Heading:** Political Parties in Congress

   Q

   A

4. **Heading:** Political Parties and State Legislatures

   Q

   A

5. **Heading:** The President as a Party Member

   Q

   A

Reading Assignment: "What Europeans Found"

3-6

WHAT EUROPEANS FOUND

The discovery of America was the world's greatest surprise. When the first Europeans came, their maps of the world left no place for America. They knew only three continents—Europe, Asia, and Africa. These seemed to be merged together into one huge "Island of the Earth." That big island was indented by lakes, and a few seas like the Mediterranean and the Western Ocean. The planet seemed covered mostly by land, and there was no room for another continent.

Columbus was not looking for a new continent. He thought he was on his way to China and India. Europeans were disappointed to find unexpected lands in their way. Still they insisted on calling the natives here the "Indians." So America was discovered by accident.

As more Europeans came and explored the unknown lands, their disappointment became surprise. They had found a world for new beginnings.

1. Christopher Columbus

The adventure that Columbus had in mind was exciting enough. He aimed to sail westward from the shores of Europe until he reached the shores of Asia. Asia was then Europe's treasure-house. It supplied peppers and spices and tea for the table, silks and gold brocade for the dresses of noble ladies and for draperies in palaces, diamonds and rubies for rings and bracelets and necklaces. Until then the main way to the Orient had been the slow, long trek overland. From Venice it might take a year to reach Peking. You would not arrive at all unless you survived the attacks of bandits, the high-mountain snows, and torrid desert heats. Even after you arrived in Asia, it was hard to bring your treasure back overland. For there were no wagon highways and you had to pack your treasure in caravans on the backs of donkeys, horses, and camels.

A direct westward voyage by sea would make all the difference. You could avoid bandits and mountains and deserts. The spacious hold of your ship would safely carry back your treasure. This was a simple and appealing idea. The wonder is why more people before Columbus did not try it.

Earlier in the 1400s a few sailors had tried. But they were not prepared for so long a voyage, and they did not know the winds. Some reached out into the Atlantic Ocean as far as the Azores and beyond. But the winds were against them and the seas rough. They all soon turned back for home.

As a determined young man Christopher Columbus decided that he would sail into the Western Ocean—to Asia and back. He had no doubt he could do it. He knew the sea, the winds, and the currents.

Early Experiences

Columbus was born in 1451 in bustling Genoa, Italy, "that noble and powerful city by the sea." He was the son of a prosperous wool-weaver. For the first 22 years of his life he lived there. He saw ships bringing rich cargo from the eastern Mediterranean where the treasures of the Orient had been taken overland. When he went to sea, he sailed in all directions where ships went at the time. Once his cargo was wool and dried fish and wine carried from Iceland and northern Ireland to Lisbon and the islands of the Azores. Then he lived for a while in the Madeira Islands off the coast of Africa. He even sailed down the steaming African coast to distant Portuguese trading posts on the Gulf of Guinea.

When he left Genoa to settle in Lisbon, Portugal, that city was "the street corner of Europe." Its deep, sheltered harbor was the point of arrival and departure, a place of exchange, for the seaborne commerce of the whole western end of the continent. From there shipments went northward to the British Isles or the North Sea, southward for trade into Africa. And, why not westward—to Asia?

There in Lisbon the single-minded young Columbus laid his plans for his grand "Enterprise of the Indies." He called it an "enterprise" because he expected it to be not just a voyage of discovery but a money-making project. "The Indies" was the name for India and the other Asian lands of the Far East. Convinced that they had a great project to sell, Christopher and his brother Bartholomew made Lisbon their headquarters.

The "Enterprise of the Indies" would not be inexpensive. Ships would have to be bought or hired, crews found and paid. Food and other supplies had to be collected for the long voyage there and back. No ordinary merchant would have the wealth and the power needed. It would take a rich monarch. There was hope of great profit, but there was also great risk. Was there a ruler bold enough to take the big gamble?

No one knew exactly what the risks might be—or even how far it was from the coast of western Europe to the coasts of Asia. No one had ever made that trip before. The questions could not be answered from experience.

The learned men disagreed in their guesses. Some said it was about 2000 miles. Others said it was two or three times that long. The leading authority was the ancient Greek geographer Ptolemy. Columbus read the best geography books he could find. We still have some of them with his own marks. He underlined the passage that said, "this sea is navigable in a very few days if the wind be fair." He believed the writers who said the distance was short, and accordingly he made his plans.

Seeking Support

Christopher and his brother traveled to the capitals of Europe trying to sell their project. The monarchs shunned Columbus's grand Enterprise of the Indies. When in 1484 King John II of Portugal asked his committee of experts if Columbus could succeed, they said it was too far to Asia and told him not to take the risk. Instead King John sent daring sailors on the long way round Africa eastward to India. In 1488 Bartholomeu Dias succeeded in rounding the Cape of Good Hope, at the southern tip of Africa. Now the eastern route to India was open. Why risk the uncertain way west when there was a sea-path to the east?

Columbus then went next door to Spain, where Queen Isabella had a mind of her own. The bold mariner awakened her interest. To finance the trip she needed money from the royal treasury, but her committee of experts refused to approve the project. She kept the impatient Columbus waiting for six years. Finally, he gave up and prepared to take ship for France. At the last moment, the court treasurer convinced Isabella the gamble was worth the risk. She now became so enthusiastic she was even prepared to pawn her jewels to help Columbus. But that was not necessary. She was told the royal treasury could pay the cost. So Queen Isabella sent Columbus a promise of royal support. She also granted all his demands for noble titles and a 10 percent share of whatever wealth came from land he might discover.

Columbus formed his enterprise in the small port of Palos, which had done something illegal. As a penalty the Queen fined it two caravels—light, swift sailboats—to go with Columbus. The caravels were the *Niña* and the *Pinta*. The third vessel of the expedition was the biggest, the *Santa Maria*, which Columbus chartered. The crew was mostly from Palos and nearby, and they were courageous and expert sailors.

The Great Voyage

With his three ships Columbus set sail from the coast of Spain on August 3, 1492. In the next weeks he proved that he was the greatest mariner of the age.

Still, it is hard to be at sea for weeks when you are not sure what—if anything—is ahead. So Columbus's men grew rebellious and reached the verge of mutiny. But Columbus was a true leader. A man taller than most, blue eyed and red haired, he was respected by his followers. He altered the records of distances they had covered so the crew would not think they had gone too far from home. He convinced them to go on. Still, on October 9, Columbus agreed that if they did not find land in three days, he would turn back. But by then there were more and more signs of land—birds in the air, leaves and flowers floating in the water.

It was not enough to know the sea. The winds were the engine that took you there and back. Others had failed because they did not know how to use the winds. They had tried going straight west from Spain. That was their mistake. Instead Columbus first had sailed south to the Canary Islands off the coast of Africa, then sailed west from there. That was where the winds blowing from the east would carry his ships straight on to his destination. Also the Canaries were on the same latitude as Japan, so if he went due west he thought he would arrive where he wanted to be.

The winds blew just as Columbus expected. This, the most important sea voyage in history, had good weather and clear sailing. At 2 o'clock in the morning on October 12, 1492, after thirty-three days at sea, a lookout sighted the white cliffs of an island in the Bahamas. The natives called it Guanahani, and Columbus named it San Salvador—Holy Savior. Columbus had discovered America—though he did not know it.

Columbus cruised about in the Caribbean Sea for several months. He landed on Cuba, which he thought and hoped might be Japan. After the *Santa Maria* was wrecked on the reef off Haiti, he built a fort on the island. They named the island Hispaniola (after Spain). He left about 40 men when he headed for home January 4, 1493. Columbus had found no great cities in his travels—but he had seen gold ornaments and found a little gold in a stream on Hispaniola. So he thought he had reached the outposts of the rich empire of Cathay (China).

By great luck Columbus did not try to sail back the way he had come. It would have been a mistake, for at that latitude the winds came from the east. Instead Columbus sailed north to about 35° north latitude. There the prevailing winds from the west blew him back to Spain.

When he arrived on March 15, 1493, he had accomplished much more then he knew. He had discovered a new world. The king and queen loaded him with honors and made his two sons pages at the court. Meanwhile he had shown sailors how to sail and where to sail so the winds would carry them to America *and back!* This made it possible for countless other ships to follow.

Columbus' Other Voyages

Three times on later voyages Columbus returned to the islands that he called the "Indies," or lands of the East. On these trips he established the first permanent settlement of Europeans in the Western Hemisphere, he skirted the shore of South America, and he explored the coast of Central America. He was always trying to prove that he had found the treasure lands of the East. But he finally reaped only misfortune and disgrace. When he returned to Spain in 1504 after his last voyage, he found Queen Isabella dying and his friends, his influence, and his reputation gone. Two years later Columbus died still believing that he had sailed to the coast of Asia.

Textbook Notes for "What Europeans Found" 3-7

1. **Title:** What Europeans Found

   Question

   Answer

2. **Heading:** 1. Christopher Columbus

   Q

   A

3. **Heading:** Early experiences

   Q

   A

4. **Heading:** Seeking support

   Q

   A

5. **Heading:** The great voyage

   Q

   A

6. **Heading:** Columbus' other voyages

   Q

   A

Chapter Three Mastery Assessment 3-8

Directions For each of the following letters in the SQ3R formula:

1. Identify the step the letter stands for.
2. Tell the important things you are to do when applying that step.

S

Q

R

R

R

ANSWERS FOR CHAPTER THREE REPRODUCIBLE ACTIVITIES

3-1 No writing required.

3-2 No writing required.

3-3 1. (Q) What would you see if you visited ancient Rome? (A) Types of dress, forms of entertainment, and what city life was like. 2. (Q) How did Roman men dress? (A) Tunics, togas, sandals. (Q) How did Roman women dress? (A) Stolas, cloaks, sandals. 3. (Q) What kinds of entertainment would you see? (A) Circuses, plays, gladiators, public baths. 4. (Q) What were the limitations of ancient Rome? (A) Hard to find places, crowded, dirty. 5. (Q) What was Rome like at night? (A) Dangerous, very dark, lots of crime, many travelers. 6. (Q) What were the hazards of travel? (A) Robbers. (Q) How did Romans plan their travel? (A) Stayed out of inns and hotels. Wealthy Romans traveled with slaves and servants for protection.

3-4 Survey, Question, Read, Recite, Review.

3-5 1. (Q) Why do we have political parties? (A) To give people a way to support or oppose government. 2. (Q) What are the names of the political parties? (A) Democratic, Republican. (Q) What do political parties do to get candidates elected? (A) Advertise, hold meetings where candidates speak, get people to vote for their candidate. 3. (Q)What do political parties do in Congress? (A) Try to get their bills passed. 4. (Q) What do political parties do in the state legislature? (A) Try to get their bills passed. 5. (Q) What does the president do as a party member? (A) Works with the party to develop bills and appoints party members to important jobs. (Q) What happens when the president does not agree with the party members on an issue? (A) They try to reach a compromise.

3-6 No writing required.

3-7 1. (Q) What did the Europeans find in America? (A) They found a world for new beginnings. 2. (Q) Who was Christopher Columbus? (A) A determined young man who liked adventure. (Q) Why did he come to America? (A) He discovered America by accident while trying to reach Asia. 3. (Q) What were his early experiences like? (A) He was the son of wealthy parents who was fascinated by the sea. He did a lot of sailing and wanted to find a route to Asia by water. He hoped to make a lot of money by doing this. 4. (Q) How did he get support for his adventure? (A) He tried to get many European monarchs to support him with money. (Q) Who gave him support? (A) Queen Isabella of Spain. (Q) What three ships did Columbus take on his adventure? (A) Niña, Pinta, Santa Maria. 5. What was his great voyage like? (A) He was a great leader. He convinced the crew to continue on. He had good weather and clear sailing. He discovered America in 1492 and returned to Spain in 1493. 6. (Q) What were Columbus' other voyages? (A) He sailed to America three more times. He started a settlement and explored the coastlines of South and Central America. At his death, he still believed that he had found Asia.

3-8 S = Survey: Read title, introduction, headings, visuals, and conclusions. Q = Question: Use the words *Who, What, Where, When,* or *How* to form questions from the title and headings. R = Read: Read to answer the questions. R = Recite: Say the questions and answers aloud until they can be recalled. R = Review: Do the same things as in the Recite step from time to time to make sure the information is remembered.

CHAPTER FOUR

Understanding Graphic Aids

CHAPTER OBJECTIVES

1. **Teach students about the graphic aids found in textbooks and other sources of information.**
2. **Teach students to interpret the information found in graphic aids.**

TITLES OF REPRODUCIBLE ACTIVITIES

4-1 Map Legend
4-2 Map Compass
4-3 Map Scale
4-4 Political and Physical Maps
4-5 Road Maps
4-6 Combining Political, Physical, and Road Maps
4-7 Weather Maps
4-8 Pictographs
4-9 Pie or Circle Graphs
4-10 Bar Graphs
4-11 Line Graphs
4-12 Diagrams
4-13 Tables
4-14 Organizational Charts
4-15 Flow Charts
4-16 Chapter Four Mastery Assessment

SUGGESTIONS FOR USING THE REPRODUCIBLE ACTIVITIES

4-1 Map Legend

Tell students that maps usually have a legend which is used to explain the symbols appearing on a map. Use the activity to introduce students to a map legend. Then have students answer the questions using the legend for the map shown.

4-2 Map Compass

Use the activity to explain a map compass. Have students complete the activity using the map compass.

4-3 Map Scale

Explain that a map scale is used to find the distance between two locations on a map. Map scales are often shown in both miles and kilometers. Demonstrate how to use the map scale. Have students answer the questions.

4-4 Political and Physical Maps

Use the activity to introduce students to political and physical maps. Bring out the unique features of each. Have students answer the questions.

4-5 Road Maps

Introduce the road map. Bring out the feature that distinguishes major highways from secondary roads. Explain how road maps are used when traveling. Have students answer the questions.

4-6 Combining Political, Physical, and Road Maps

Review the use of a legend, compass, and scale. Have students use the map to answer the questions about the state of California.

4-7 Weather Maps

Introduce the weather map. Explain how weather maps are used to interpret present weather conditions and predict future conditions. Have students answer the questions.

4-8 Pictographs

Tell students that another way to show information is with graphs. Explain that graphs show the relationship between two or more things. Tell students you will be teaching them about four types of graphs: pictographs, pie or circle, bar, and line. Use this activity to introduce students to pictographs. Then have students answer the questions.

4-9 Pie or Circle Graphs

Tell students the term *pie graph* is used because this type of graph looks like a pie divided into slices. Emphasize that the parts must add up to 100%. Have students complete the activity.

4-10 Bar Graphs

Show students the different parts of a bar graph. Review the five steps for reading a bar graph. Have students complete the activity.

4-11 Line Graphs

Explain that line graphs are used to show trends over a period of time. Review the five steps for reading a line graph. Have students complete the activity.

4-12 Diagrams

Use the activity to introduce diagrams. Bring out that diagrams show how parts go together or how some object or thing works. Emphasize the importance of the key. Then have students answer the questions.

4-13 Tables

Use the activity to introduce tables. Explain the importance of columns and column headings. Review the three steps for reading a table. Have students complete the activity.

4-14 Organizational Charts

Introduce organizational charts with this activity. Explain how boxes and lines are used to present information and show relationships. Have students answer the questions.

4-15 Flow Charts

Introduce flow charts using this activity. Bring out that flow charts are used to show a process by which something works or occurs. Point out the significance of the arrows. Have students answer the questions.

4-16 Chapter Four Mastery Assessment

Have students complete this assessment at any point you believe they have learned to interpret graphic aids. Review the results of the assessment with the students. Provide additional instruction as necessary.

Map Legend

4-1

To read a map you need to use the **map legend.** The legend is usually located near the bottom of a map. It contains information that explains the symbols you see on a map. The legend on one map is different from the legend on another map because each map contains different kinds of information. The map legend is sometimes called by another name, the **map key.**

Here is a map with its legend. The legend tells you what the symbols on this map mean. This legend will help you only with this map. Use the map and legend to answer the questions that follow.

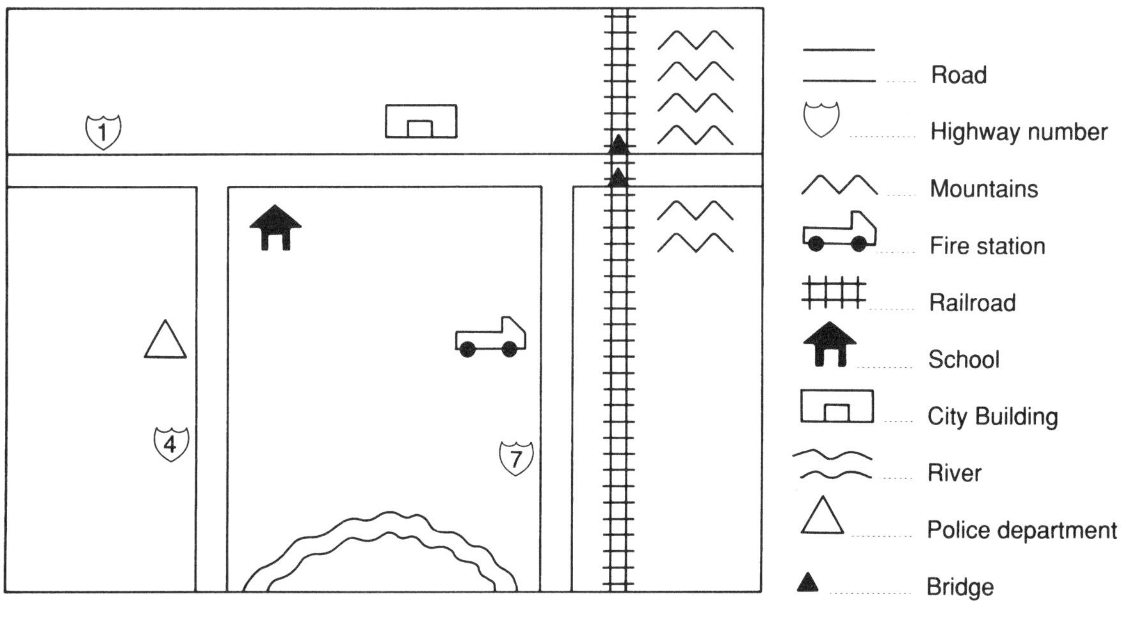

1. Next to which highway is the police department? ________________
2. How many fire stations are there? ________________
3. Draw the symbol for a railroad. ________________
4. How many highways are there? ________________
5. Which highway is the longest? ________________
6. Do the railroad tracks cross the river? ________________
7. Next to which highway is the fire station? ________________
8. Along which highway is the city building? ________________
9. Which highway has a bridge across it? ________________
10. Is there a bridge across the river? ________________
11. Which two highways run in the same direction? ________________
12. Near which two highways will you find a school? ________________

Map Compass

To tell directions on a map, you need to know how to use the **map compass.** The map compass tells you north (N), south (S), east (E), west (W), and the directions in between: northeast (NE), southeast (SE), northwest (NW), and southwest (SW). Use the map of Ohio and the compass to answer the questions that follow.

Use the compass to tell in what direction you would travel to go from Columbus to the following cities.

1. Freemont ____________________
2. Greenville ____________________
3. Defiance ____________________
4. Athens ____________________

In what direction would you travel if you went from

5. Cleveland to Cincinnati? ____________________
6. Portsmouth to Athens? ____________________

Map Scale **4-3**

The **map scale** tells distance on a map. Sometimes it tells the distance only in miles, sometimes only in kilometers, and sometimes in both miles and kilometers. You can use the map scale to tell how far it is from one place to another.

Here is a map of Oregon containing cities and a map scale.

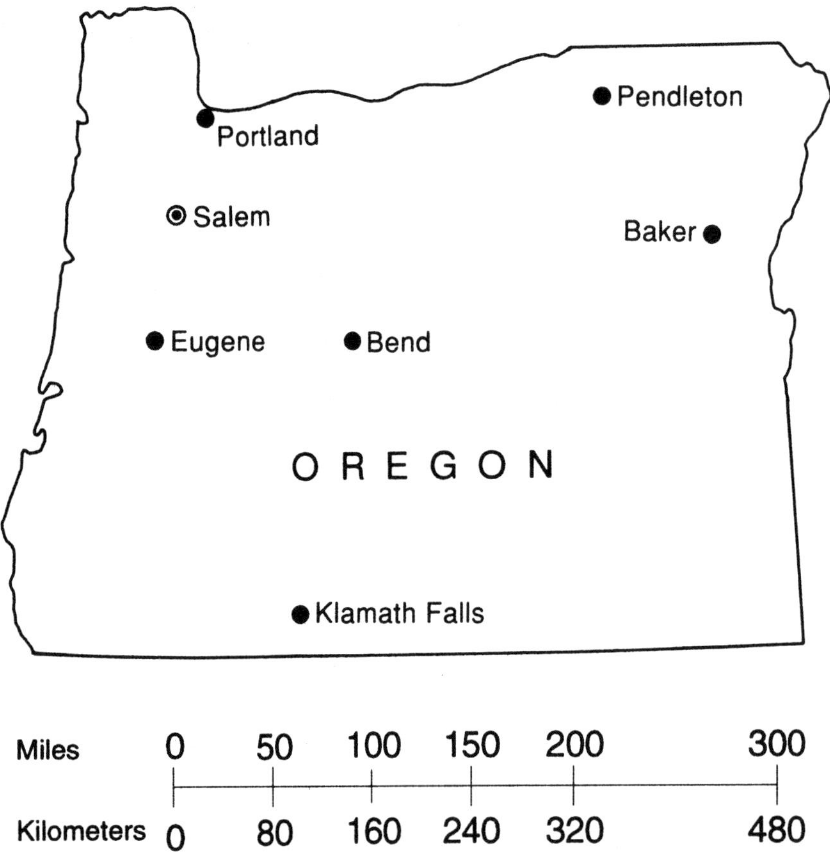

You can find the distance between any two cities by using the map scale. Place the edge of a piece of paper between any two cities shown on the map. Make a mark on the paper by each city. Then lay the paper on the scale to find out how far it is between the two marks. This will tell you how far it is between the two cities.

How far is it between

1. Salem and Klamath Falls in miles? ________________
2. Portland and Bend in kilometers? ________________
3. Eugene and Pendleton in miles? ________________
4. Bend and Salem in kilometers? ________________

Political and Physical Maps

A **political** map has lines that show political or government boundaries. Look at the political map of South America, which shows the countries on this continent.

A **physical** map shows the features of the earth's surface such as mountains, highlands, plateaus, deserts, and major bodies of water. Look at the physical map of South America and find these features. No political boundaries are shown.

Which type of map would you use to:

1. identify the provinces in Canada? ____________________
2. identify major mountain ranges? ____________________
3. write a report on the major oceans in the world? ____________________
4. answer a question about the new countries in Eastern Europe? ____________

Road Maps

4-5

A **road map** shows the major highways and the secondary roads for a geographical area. The major highways are identified with dark lines and the secondary roads with light lines. Both types of roads have symbols showing the number or name of the highway or road. Road maps are used to show how to get from one place to another. Here is a sample road map.

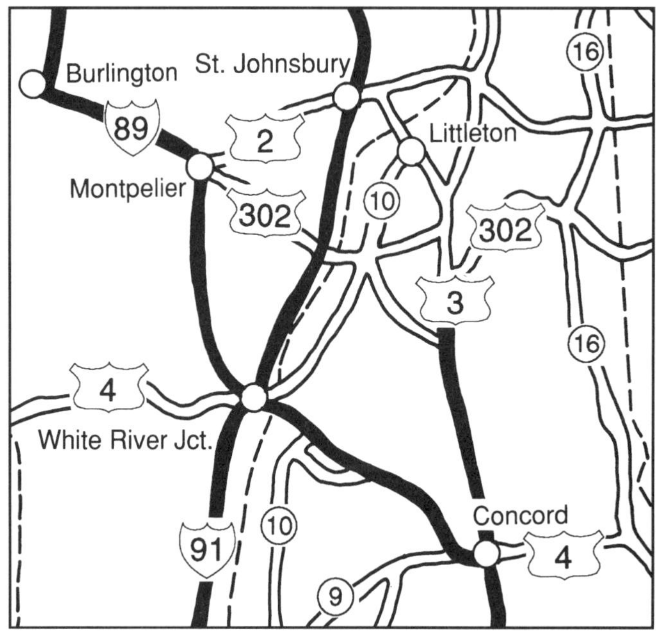

1. What do dark lines identify? ______________________________

2. Light lines? ______________________________

3. What route would you take to travel between Burlington and Concord? ______________

4. What direct route takes you from Concord to Littleton? ______________________

Combining Political, Physical, and Road Maps

4-6

Here is a map of California that combines the features from political, physical, and road maps. It has a legend, compass, and scale. Use the map to answer the questions.

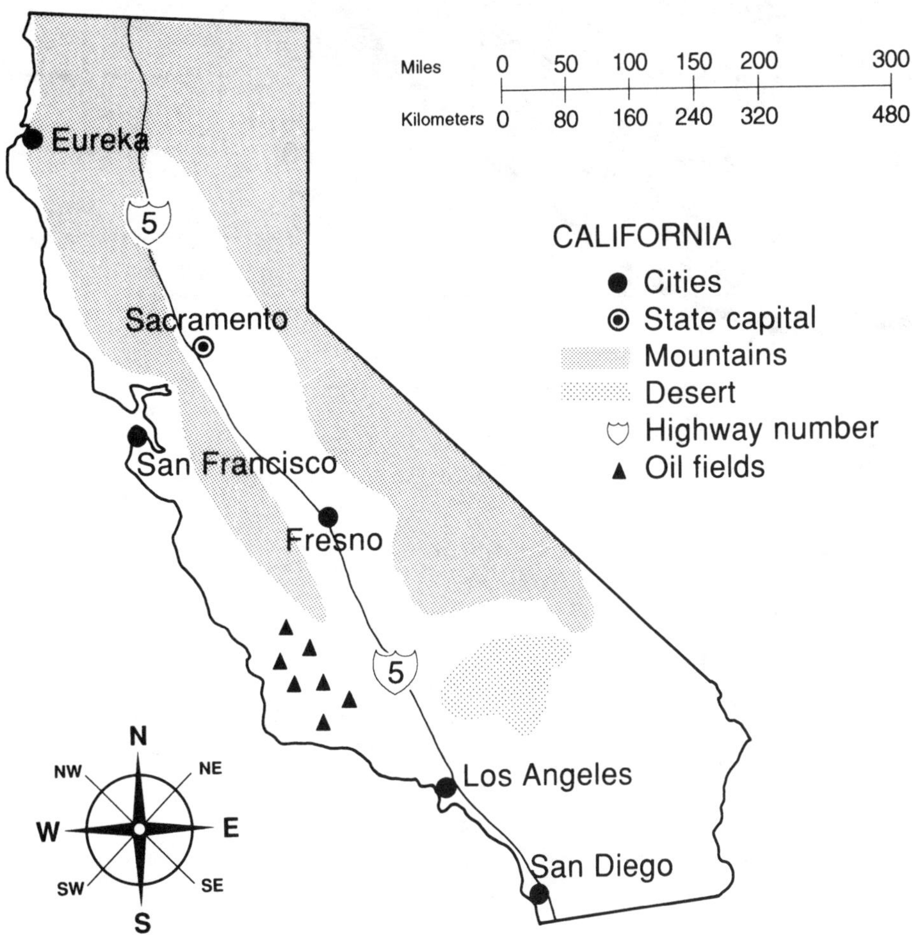

1. Between which two cities are oil fields located? ____________________

2. What is the distance in kilometers between San Francisco and Los Angeles? __________

3. What is the state capital? ____________________

4. In which direction would you travel from San Francisco to Fresno? __________

Weather Maps

Maps can be used to tell information about the weather. Use the legend and compass to answer the questions.

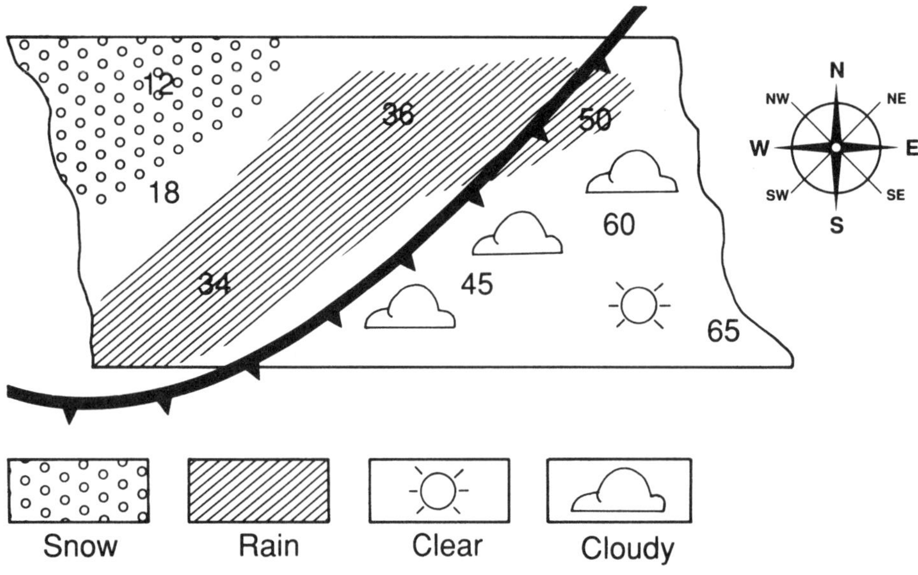

Snow Rain Clear Cloudy

Dividing line between fronts

► Direction of front

Numbers show temperatures

What is the predicted weather for these areas?

1. SE ____________________

2. NE ____________________

3. NW ____________________

4. SW ____________________

5. In which area is the coldest temperature? ____________________

6. In which area is the warmest temperature? ____________________

7. What will the weather be like in the SE area in a day or two? ____________________

Pictographs

4-8

Graphs show how two or more things go together. Graphs make difficult and complex things easier to understand. There are four types of graphs you need to know how to interpret: pictographs, pie or circle graphs, bar graphs, and line graphs. All of these are used in social studies, science, and mathematics textbooks.

Pictographs use pictures to show information. Each picture stands for an amount of something. A pictograph has a title that tells you what it shows. It also has a key that explains what each picture stands for. Here is a pictograph. Study it and answer the questions.

Games Won by NFL Teams

Dolphins
Bears
Giants
Cardinals
Saints
Rams

Key: = game won

1. Which team won the most games? ______________________

2. Which team won the fewest games? ______________________

3. How many games did the Cardinals win? ______________________

4. How many games did the Bears win? ______________________

5. How many more games did the Bears win than the Cardinals? ______________________

6. Which two teams won the same number of games? ______________________

7. How many teams won more games than the Bears? ______________________

8. How many teams won fewer games than the Giants? ______________________

9. What does stand for? ______________________

10. Where did you look to find out what stands for? ______________________

11. What is the title of this pictograph? ______________________

Pie or Circle Graphs **4-9**

Some graphs use a circle to show the relationship between the parts of something and the whole thing. This type of graph is called either a **pie graph** or a **circle graph.** The name *pie graph* is used because the graph looks like a pie divided into slices. Each part of a pie or circle graph shows how much of the whole it stands for. The parts must equal the whole and must add up to 100 percent.

Study the following pie or circle graph and answer the questions.

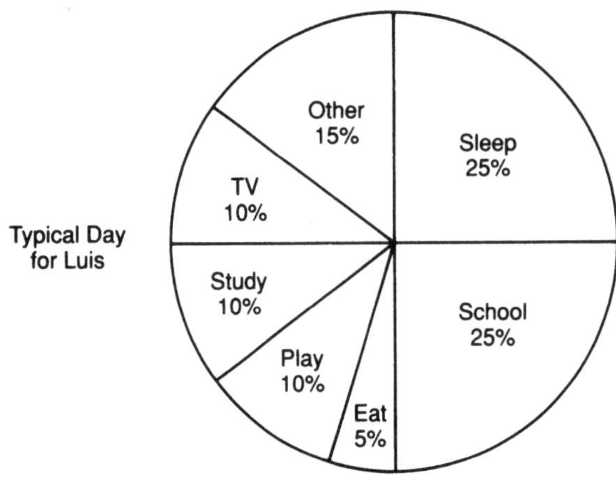

What percentage of the day does Luis spend:

1. sleeping? __________
2. studying? __________
3. in school? __________
4. watching TV? __________
5. playing? __________
6. both at school and studying? __________
7. playing and watching TV? __________
8. What does Luis spend 5% of his day doing? __________
9. Does Luis spend more time sleeping than watching TV, studying, and playing combined?

   ____
10. Does Luis spend more time at school than he does sleeping? __________

Bar Graphs

Bar graphs use bars to show the relationships between sets of facts. The bar graph has a title at the top and labels on the left-hand side and bottom. On the left side of the graph there is a number line. The height of each bar shows how much the bar stands for. Look at the following bar graph.

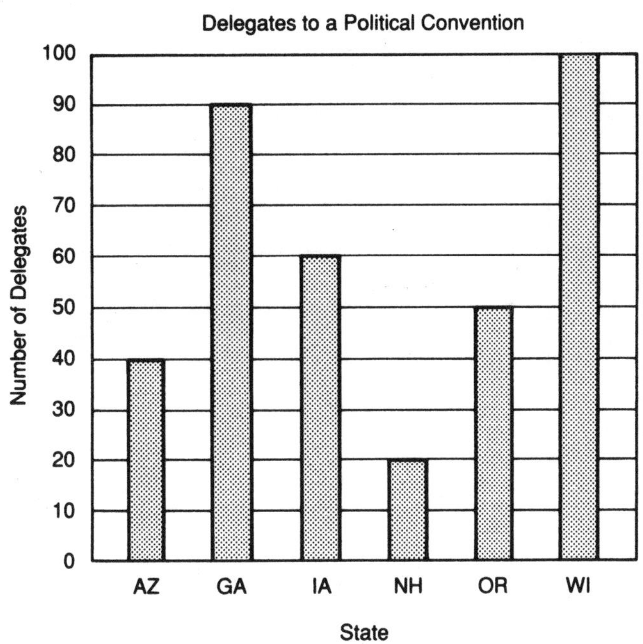

To read a bar graph you need to do the following:

1. Read the title to learn what it is about.
2. Read the label at the bottom to learn what the bars stand for.
3. Read the label on the left to learn what the numbers stand for.
4. Look at the height of any one bar to learn about a specific thing.
5. Look at the height of two or more bars to make comparisons between things.

Answer these questions:

1. What is this bar graph about?
2. What do the bars stand for?
3. What do the numbers stand for?
4. How many delegates came from Iowa (IA)?
5. Which state sent the most delegates?
6. How many more delegates did IA send than NH?

Line Graphs

4-11

Line graphs are used to show trends over a period of time. The line graph has a title at the top and labels on the left-hand side and the bottom. On the left side of the line graph there is a number line. Dots are used to show how much there is of something. The dots are connected by a line. The line shows how a trend is developing or how things are changing. Look at the following line graph.

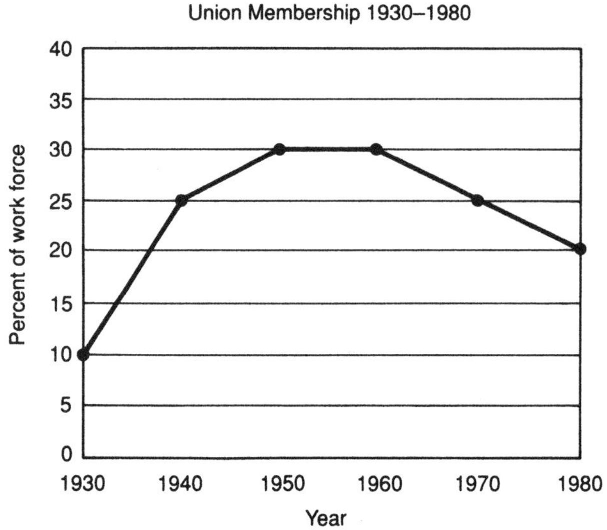

To read a line graph you need to do the following:

1. Read the title to learn what it is about.
2. Read the label at the bottom to learn what the dots stand for.
3. Read the label on the left to learn what the numbers stand for.
4. Look at any one dot to learn about a specific thing.
5. Look at the line to see the trend or how things are changing.

Answer these questions:

1. What is this line graph about?
2. What do the dots stand for?
3. What do the numbers on the left side stand for?
4. What percent of the work force belonged to unions in 1930?
5. What happened to union membership between 1930 and 1950?
6. In what ten-year period was there the greatest increase in union membership?
7. In what year did union membership begin to drop?

Diagrams are drawings of an object or thing. A diagram shows the parts of the object or thing. Often a diagram shows how the parts go together or how the object or thing works. Next to the diagram is a key. The key helps you understand the diagram. Look at the following diagram and key. Use the diagram and key to answer the questions.

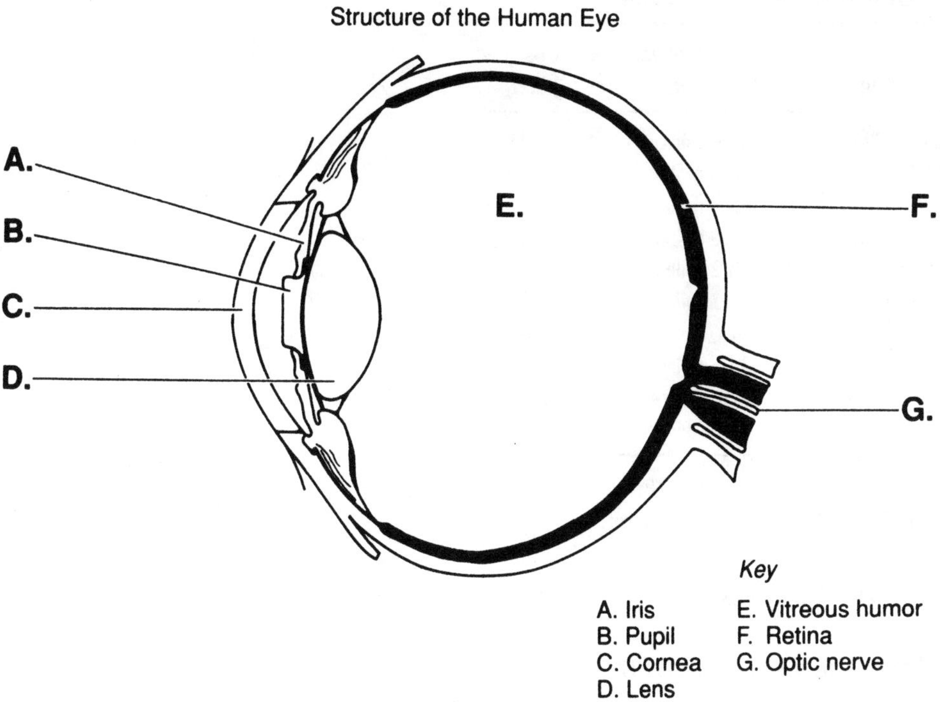

1. What is the title of this diagram?

2. What can you learn from studying this diagram?

3. How many parts of the eye are labeled?

4. What is the largest part?

5. What does G identify?

Tables

Tables are used to show facts that would be difficult to understand quickly and accurately if they were presented in written form. A table has a title that explains its purpose. In the table you will find columns. Each column has a heading that tells what facts you will find in that column. Look at the following table.

Total Campaign Spending, 1952–1988

Year	*Estimated Spending*	*Votes Cast for President*	*Cost per Voter*
1952	$140 million	61.6 million	$2.28
1956	155 million	62.0 million	2.50
1960	175 million	68.8 million	2.54
1964	200 million	70.6 million	2.83
1968	300 million	73.2 million	4.10
1972	425 million	77.7 million	5.47
1976	540 million	81.6 million	6.62
1980	1.2 billion	86.5 million	13.87
1984	1.8 billion	92.6 million	19.38
1988	3.0 billion	91.6 million	32.75

Source: Magruder, *American Government* (Englewood Cliffs, NJ: Prentice Hall, 1990). Used with permission.

To read a table you need to do the following:

1. Read the title to learn what the table is about.
2. Look at each column heading to learn what information the table contains.
3. Look in each column to get specific facts.

Answer these questions:

1. What is the title of this table?
2. What information is provided in the second column?
3. In the third column?
4. In the fourth column?
5. In which column should you look to find the number of people who voted for a president?
6. In what year was the most money spent on campaigns?
7. In what year was the cost per voter the least?
8. In what year did campaign spending first go over $1 billion?
9. What is the first year for which information is given on cost per voter?

Organizational Charts

Organizational charts are used to show how things are organized. Information is presented in boxes. Each box is labeled to show what it represents. Lines are used to show how the boxes are related.

Look at the following organizational chart. It shows how the U.S. government is organized to do its work. The boxes contain facts about the government. The lines show how the facts go together. By studying the chart you can see how the government works.

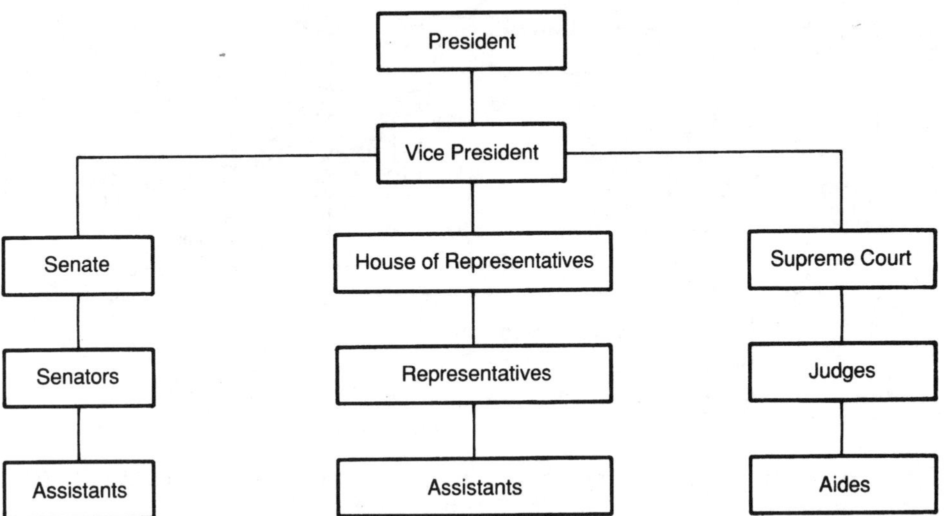

Use the chart to answer these questions:

1. Who is the highest ranking official in the United States government?

2. Who works in the Senate?

3. Who works in the House of Representatives?

4. Who works in the Supreme Court?

5. What official is directly below the president?

6. Where do aides work?

7. For whom do assistants work?

Flow charts are used to show a process by which something works or occurs. Information is presented with drawings and a series of arrows. Statements are found next to the drawings to show what is occurring at that point. The arrows show the direction or order in which the process occurs.

Look at the following flow chart, which shows how a nuclear reactor works. Read the title and the statements, and study the drawings. Then use the arrows to learn the process.

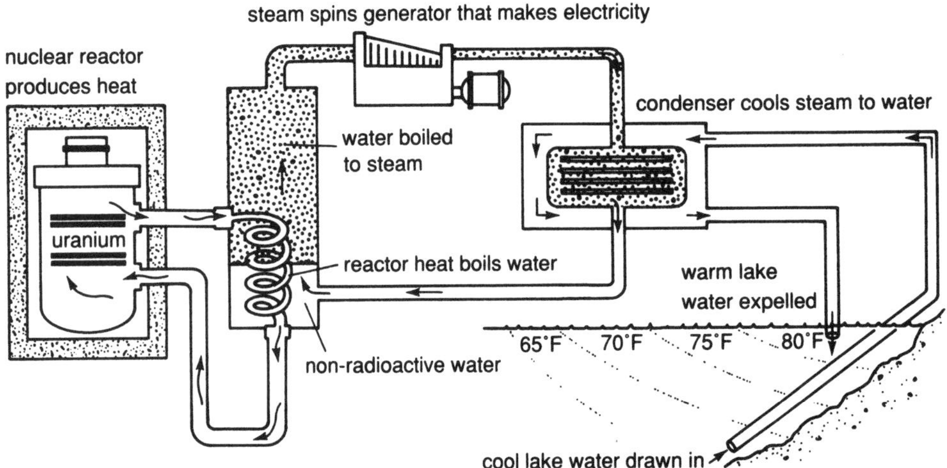

Simplified flow chart of a nuclear reactor. Laurel Cook, Boston, MA. Adapted from *1990 Information Please Almanac* (Boston: Houghton Mifflin, 1990), p. 377.

Answer these questions:

1. What is the title?
2. What process is being shown?
3. What creates the heat in the nuclear reactor?
4. What is the heat used for?
5. What spins the generator?
6. What makes the electricity?
7. What changes the steam back to water?
8. Where does the water come from for the cooling process?
9. Where does the warm water go?

Chapter Four Mastery Assessment **4-16**

Directions Show what you have learned about interpreting visual aids by writing an answer for each of the following:

1. Tell what each type of map shows:
   a. Political
   b. Physical
   c. Road
   d. Weather
2. What is each of the following used for on a map?
   a. Legend
   b. Compass
   c. Scale
3. What is used to show how much there is of something in a pictograph?
4. What is another name for a circle graph?
5. What does the height of the bar show in a bar graph?
6. What type of graph is used to show trends over a period of time?
7. What type of drawing shows the parts of some object or thing?
8. What is used to show facts in columns?
9. What type of chart is used to show how things are organized?
10. What type of chart is used to show how something works?

ANSWERS FOR CHAPTER FOUR REPRODUCIBLE ACTIVITIES

4-1 1. 4. 2. 1. 3. #. 4. 3. 5. 1. 6. No. 7. 7. 8. 1. 9. 1. 10. No. 11. 4,7. 12. 1,4.

4-2 1. N. 2. W. 3. NW. 4. SE. 5. SW. 6. NE

4-3 1. 200. 2. 210. 3. 240. 4. 160.

4-4 1. Political 2. Physical 3. Physical 4. Political

4-5 1. Major highways. 2. Secondary roads. 3. 89 or any route that works. 4. 3.

4-6 1. San Francisco and Los Angeles. 2. 580 kilometers. 3. Sacramento. 4. SE.

4-7 1. Clear. 2. Cloudy and rain. 3. Snow. 4. Rain. 5. NW. 6. SE. 7. Cloudy, possible rain turning to snow, colder.

4-8 1. Dolphins. 2. Saints. 3. 7. 4. 9. 5. 2. 6. Giants and Rams. 7. 3. 8. 2. 9. Two games won. 10. Key. 11. Games won by NFL teams.

4-9 1. 25%. 2. 10%. 3. 25%. 4. 10%. 5. 10%. 6. 35%. 7. 20%. 8. Eating. 9. No. 10. No.

4-10 1. Delegates to a political convention. 2. States. 3. Number of delegates. 4. 60. 5. Wisconsin. 6. 40.

4-11 1. Union membership during the years 1930–1980. 2. Years. 3. Percent of work force. 4. 10%. 5. Increased. 6. 1930–1940. 7. 1960.

4-12 1. Structure of the Human Eye. 2. Names of parts of the human eye. 3. 7. 4. Vitreous humor. 5. Optic nerve.

4-13 1. Total Campaign Spending, 1952–1988. 2. Estimated spending. 3. Votes cast for president. 4. Cost per voter. 5. 3rd column "Votes Cast for President." 6. 1988. 7. 1952. 8. 1980. 9. 1952.

4-14 1. President. 2. Senators and assistants. 3. Representatives and assistants. 4. Judges and aides. 5. Vice-president. 6. Supreme Court. 7. Senators and representatives.

4-15 1. Simplified flow chart of a nuclear reactor. 2. The process of using a nuclear reactor to generate electricity. 3. Uranium. 4. Boil water. 5. steam. 6. Generator. 7. Condenser. 8. From the lake. 9. Back to the lake.

4-16 1. (a) Political or government boundaries. (b) Features of the earth's surface. (c) Major highways and secondary roads. (d) Major weather systems. 2. (a) To explain the symbols on a map. (b) Tells directions on a map. (c) Tells distance on a map. 3. Pictures. 4. Pie graph. 5. How much of something. 6. Line graph. 7. Diagram. 8. Table. 9. Organizational chart. 10. Flow chart.

CHAPTER FIVE

Remembering Important Information

CHAPTER OBJECTIVES

1. **Teach students how to select information to be remembered.**
2. **Teach students how to use strategies to remember information.**

TITLES OF REPRODUCIBLE ACTIVITIES

5-1 Selecting Information to Be Remembered
5-2 Using Visualization
5-3 Using Categorization
5-4 Using Repetition
5-5 Using Rhymes
5-6 Using Abbreviations
5-7 Using Acronyms
5-8 Using Acronymic Sentences
5-9 Chapter Five Mastery Assessment

SUGGESTIONS FOR USING THE REPRODUCIBLE ACTIVITIES

5-1 Selecting Information to Be Remembered

Elaborate on the four things students should do to select the information they need to remember for a test. Then tell students what will be covered on the next test. Then have students write information they need to remember from their textbook reading assignments, class notes, and any handouts you have provided.

5-2 Using Visualization

Help students understand that visualization involves creating one or more mental images or pictures, which are later used to recall information. Emphasize that mental images serve as a place to collect and hold together facts to be remembered. Tell students that if they include names, dates, and places in their images, they will be able to remember a substantial collection of information. Have students find a reading assignment and use what they learned about visualization to complete the activity.

5-3 Using Categorization

Tell students that categorization involves organizing items to be remembered into categories. Lead students through the example, which shows how categorization can be used to remember the items to buy at a store. Then have students complete the activity.

5-4 Using Repetition

Tell students that repetition involves reading, saying, and writing information to be remembered. Lead students through the four steps of repetition. Then have them complete the activity in which they use repetition to remember information for a test.

5-5 Using Rhymes

Introduce the examples of rhymes used to remember information. Ask students to provide examples of rhymes they have used to remember information. Then have them complete the activity in which they write a rhyme to remember information for a test.

5-6 Using Abbreviations

Show students that abbreviations are formed using the first letter of each word to be remembered. Review the example for UFO. Help students understand that abbreviations are not pronounced but are recited as letters. Tell students abbreviations are best used when information needs to be remembered in order. Then have students complete the activity.

5-7 Using Acronyms

Define an acronym as a word created from the first letter of other words. Point out that an acronym does not have to be a real word, but must be a word that can be pronounced. Tell students acronyms are best used when information does not need to be remembered in a certain order. Review how HOMES was formed. Then have students complete the page.

5-8 Using Acronymic Sentences

Tell students that acronymic sentences are sentences that are made up of words that begin with the first letter of each word to be remembered. Use the example provided for remembering the order of the planets going outward from the sun. Then have students complete the activity to learn how acronymic sentences can be created to remember information that either does or does not need to be remembered in a certain order.

5-9 Chapter Five Mastery Assessment

Have students complete this assessment at any point you believe they have learned to use the remembering strategies presented in this chapter. Review the results of the assessment with the students. Provide additional instruction as necessary.

Selecting Information to Be Remembered

5-1

Here is what to do to select the information you need to remember for a test.

- Ask your teacher what will be covered on the test.
- Read the text assignments and take notes on the important information to be remembered.
- Look at your class notes and underline or highlight the important information to be remembered.
- Look at any handouts given to you by your teacher and underline or highlight the important information to be remembered.

Write what your teacher tells you will be covered on the next test.

Write the information you need to remember from your textbook, class notes, and handouts.

Using Visualization 5-2

Visualization means creating a picture in your mind. Visualization is a good way to remember things that are easy to picture. When you are reading, try to create a picture in your mind that will help you remember the information.

Find a textbook in which you have a reading assignment and do the following:

1. Begin reading your assignment.
2. When you read something you think is important to remember for a test, stop and put the book down.
3. Create a picture in your mind of what you need to remember.
4. Draw the picture here. You may need to draw more than one picture.

5. To make sure your picture is complete, reread the information in the textbook.
6. If your picture is not complete, add what is necessary to complete it.

Using Categorization

5-3

Here is how to remember a list of things. Suppose you want to remember to buy the following nine items at a store: ruler, raisins, pen, magazine, juice, potato chips, marker, apple, newspaper. You can remember the items by organizing them into categories. Look at how this is done.

Things to Read	*Things to Write With*	*Snacks*
magazine	pen	potato chips
newspaper	ruler	raisins
	marker	apple
		juice

When you organize items to be remembered into categories, you are using a remembering technique called **categorization.**

Read these items: handle bars, couch, bat, table, gears, chair, pitcher, ball, lamp, glove, brakes, wheel. Think of categories into which they can be grouped. Write the name of each category. Below each category write the items that belong in that category.

Using Repetition

5-4

When you read, say, and write information a number of times to remember it you are using **repetition**. Here is how repetition is done:

Repetition Steps

1. Read the information aloud.

2. Close your eyes and repeat the information aloud.

3. Write the information from memory.

4. Repeat the steps at least three times or until you can remember the information without error.

Write the information you need to remember for a test. Use the repetition steps to help you remember the information.

Using Rhymes

5-5

Rhymes are another way to remember information. Here are two rhymes that many students use to remember information:

In fourteen hundred ninety-two
    Columbus sailed the ocean blue.

Thirty days hath September,
    April, June, and November.

You do not have to be a poet to make rhymes. Let your imagination run wild. If you can create a rhyme that works for you, use it. If you cannot create a rhyme, use one of the other ways you are learning to remember information.

List the information you want to remember for a test.

Select one item from your list and write a rhyme that will help you remember it. Write it here:

Using Abbreviations **5-6**

Another way to remember information is by using **abbreviations.** Abbreviations are formed using the first letter of each word to be remembered. This is a good way to remember information that has to be remembered in a certain order. You do not pronounce an abbreviation; you simply recite the letters in order. For example, UFO is an abbreviation used to remember Unidentified Flying Object.

Write the abbreviation for each of the following:

1. National Broadcasting Company
2. Disc Jockey
3. Mind Your Own Business
4. Intelligence Quotient
5. Write a set of words you need to remember for a test.

6. Write an abbreviation that will help you remember the set of words you wrote.

Using Acronyms

5-7

An **acronym** is a word formed using the first letter of a set of words. An acronym does not have to be a real word, but must be a word that can be pronounced. This is a good way to remember information that does not have to be remembered in a certain order. For example, here are the names of the five Great Lakes which do not have to be remembered in a certain order:

Michigan **Erie** **Superior** **Ontario** **Huron**

If you rearrange the order of the names of the lakes, you can use the first letter of each name to form the acronym **HOMES**. In this acronym, **H** stands for **Huron, O** for **Ontario, M** for **Michigan, E** for **Erie,** and **S** for **Superior.**

Write a list of words you want to remember for a test or other assignment. Try to form an acronym to remember the words. If you cannot form an acronym, try using one of the other ways you learned to remember information.

Words to remember:

Acronym or other way to remember:

Using Acronymic Sentences **5-8**

Acronymic sentences are formed by using words that begin with the first letter of each word you want to remember. For example, you can remember the order of the planets in our solar system according to their position from the sun by creating the acronymic sentence "My (Mercury) very (Venus) earthy (Earth) mother (Mars) just (Jupiter) served (Saturn) us (Uranus) nine (Neptune) pizzas (Pluto)."

Create an acronymic sentence for each of the following. In the first case you will have to remember the information in the order given. In the second case you can rearrange the information in any order to make it easier to create an acronymic sentence.

1. The first seven presidents of the United States in the order in which they served: Washington, Adams, Jefferson, Madison, Monroe, Adams, Jackson.

2. The eight parts of speech: adverb, conjunction, noun, adjective, verb, preposition, pronoun, interjection.

3. List some words you want to remember for a test or other assignment:

4. Write an acronymic sentence that will help you remember the words.

Chapter Five Mastery Assessment 5-9

See what you have learned about remembering information:

1. What are four things to do to select important information to remember for a test?

2. What is visualization?

3. How does categorization help you remember information?

4. Write the four steps in the repetition procedure.

5. Do you need to be a poet to create rhymes?

6. How are abbreviations formed?

7. What is an acronym?

8. How are acronymic sentences formed?

ANSWERS FOR CHAPTER FIVE REPRODUCIBLE ACTIVITIES

5-1 Responses will vary.

5-2 Responses will vary.

5-3

Bicycle Parts	*Furniture*	*Baseball*
handle bars	couch	bat
gears	table	pitcher
brakes	lamp	ball
wheel	chair	glove

5-4 Responses will vary.

5-5 Responses will vary.

5-6 1. NBC. 2. DJ. 3. MYOB. 4. IQ. 5. and 6. Responses will vary.

5-7 Responses will vary.

5-8 Responses will vary.

5-9
1. Ask your teacher what will be covered on the test.
   Read text assignments and take notes on important information.
   Underline or highlight important information in class notes.
   Underline or highlight important information in handouts.
2. Creating a picture in your mind.
3. By organizing information into categories.
4. Read the information aloud.
   Close eyes and repeat information aloud.
   Write information from memory.
   Repeat steps at least three more times.
5. No.
6. By using the first letter of each word to be remembered.
7. A word formed using the first letter of a set of words.
8. By using words that begin with the first letter of each word to be remembered.

CHAPTER SIX

Preparing for and Taking Tests

CHAPTER OBJECTIVES

1. **Teach students a five-day strategy for preparing to take tests.**
2. **Teach students strategies for taking different types of tests.**

TITLES OF REPRODUCIBLE ACTIVITIES

6-1 Getting Ready for Tests
6-2 Five-Day Test Preparation Plan
6-3 Things to Do When Taking Tests
6-4 Learning about Multiple-Choice Tests
6-5 Guidelines for Taking Multiple-Choice Tests
6-6 Practice Taking a Multiple-Choice Test
6-7 Guidelines for Taking True/False Tests
6-8 Practice Taking a True/False Test
6-9 Guidelines for Taking Matching Tests
6-10 Practice Taking Matching Tests
6-11 Guidelines for Taking Completion Tests
6-12 Practice Taking a Completion Test
6-13 Understanding Direction Words in Essay Tests
6-14 Guidelines for Taking Essay Tests
6-15 Practice Taking an Essay Test
6-16 Chapter Six Mastery Assessment

SUGGESTIONS FOR USING THE REPRODUCIBLE ACTIVITIES

6-1 Getting Ready for Tests

Tell students they will be learning how to get ready for tests. Discuss the four things students should do. Then have students write a statement telling about each.

6-2 Five-Day Test Preparation Plan

Have students read the Five-Day Test Preparation Plan. Then call upon different students to explain what is done on different study days. Then have students write statements telling what they would do on each of the five days.

6-3 Things to Do When Taking Tests

Have students read the five things to do when taking tests. Have students compare these with what they often do. Conclude by having students write statements about the five things to do.

6-4 Learning about Multiple-Choice Tests

Use the activity to show examples of the two types of multiple-choice items students will encounter on tests. Then have students complete the activity.

6-5 Guidelines for Taking Multiple-Choice Tests

Have students take notes as you explain each guideline.

6-6 Practice Taking a Multiple-Choice Test

Have students follow the guidelines they learned as they take the practice multiple-choice test. Allow five minutes for the test. Go over the answers and have students rate their performance using the scale provided.

6-7 Guidelines for Taking True/False Tests

Have students take notes as you explain each guideline.

6-8 Practice Taking a True/False Test

Have students follow the guidelines they learned as they take the practice true/false test. Allow five minutes for the test. Go over the answers and have students rate their performance using the scale provided.

6-9 Guidelines for Taking Matching Tests

Take students through the sample matching test. Then have students take notes as you explain each guideline.

6-10 Practice Taking Matching Tests

Have students take the practice tests. Allow five minutes. Go over the answers and have students rate their performance using the scale provided.

6-11 Guidelines for Taking Completion Tests

Use the test items to show how missing parts can appear anywhere in a statement. Then have students take notes as you explain each guideline.

6-12 Practice Taking a Completion Test

Have students follow the guidelines they learned as they take the practice Completion test. Allow five minutes for the test. Go over the answers and have students rate their performance using the scale provided.

6-13 Understanding Direction Words in Essay Tests

Use this activity to introduce students to direction words they will often find in items on essay tests. After discussion, have students write summaries that tell what the direction words mean.

6-14 Guidelines for Taking Essay Tests

Have students take notes as you explain each guideline.

6-15 Practice Taking an Essay Test

Have students answer the test item. Remind them to attend to the direction word and follow the guidelines they learned for taking an essay test. Allow 10 minutes. Review answer with students.

6-16 Chapter Six Mastery Assessment

Have students complete this assessment at any point you feel they have learned how to prepare for and take tests. Review the results of the assessment with the students. Provide additional instruction as necessary.

Getting Ready for Tests

6-1

You can get better grades on your tests if you do the following:

1. Ask your teacher to explain what will be on the test. Also ask what will not be on the test. This way you know exactly what you need to study for the test.
2. Review your textbook notes to be sure they are complete. Compare your notes with those taken by other students. Ask your teacher to clarify anything you do not understand.
3. Review your class notes to be sure they are complete. Compare your class notes with notes taken by other students. Ask your teacher to clarify anything you do not understand.
4. To learn all you need to know to do well on a test and get a good grade, you need to begin to prepare early. Schedule your time so you will be able to start preparing five days before the test is given.

What four things should you do to get ready for your next test?

1.

2.

3.

4.

Five-Day Test Preparation Plan **6-2**

Here is a five-day plan you should use to prepare for a test. The five-day plan shows what you should do each day to get ready for the test. If you follow the five-day plan, each day you will find yourself more ready to take the test.

Here is what you need to do each day:

Day Five	Read the notes you took in class. Read the notes you took from your textbook. Read over all the handouts provided by your teacher. On this day you should identify all the important information you must know and remember for the test. Highlight or underline the important information in your notes.
Day Four	Use the strategies you have learned, such as visualization, categorization, repetition, rhymes, abbreviations, acronyms, and acronymic sentences, to help you remember the important information you identified on Day Five.
Day Three	Rehearse the information using the remembering strategies you developed.
Day Two	Rehearse again. Also make a list of questions you think your teacher will ask on the test. Write answers for these questions.
Day One	This is the day you take the test. Rehearse the information while eating breakfast or riding to school.

What should you do on each day of the Five-Day Plan?

Day Five:

Day Four:

Day Three:

Day Two:

Day One:

Things to Do When Taking Tests

6-3

Here are five things you should do to improve your score on any test.

1. Read the test directions carefully. Ask your teacher to explain any directions or words you do not understand.
2. Look over the entire test to see how much there is to do.
3. Decide how much time you should spend answering each question. Plan to spend more time on those questions that count for the most points.
4. Answer the easiest questions first.
5. Review your answers to be sure they are correct.

What five things should you do when taking a test?

1.

2.

3.

4.

5.

Learning about Multiple-Choice Tests **6-4**

There are two types of multiple-choice test items. Both have a stem and a number of answer choices.

The first type has an incomplete statement followed by possible answers to complete the statement. Your job is to identify the answer that correctly completes the statement. Here is an example of this type of item.

There are ______________ months in a year. (Stem)
(Answer choices)
a. 9
b. 12
c. 52
d. 7

The second type has a question followed by possible answers. Your job is to identify the correct answer to the question. Here is an example of this type of item.

How many months are there in a year? (Stem)
(Answer choices)
a. 9
b. 12
c. 52
d. 7

Use the information in the box to write multiple-choice test items. Write one item for each type.

Year: 1492.
Event: Columbus discovered America.

1.
   a.
   b.
   c.
   d.

2.
   a.
   b.
   c.
   d.

Guidelines for Taking Multiple-Choice Tests

6-5

There are a number of things you can do to choose the correct answer for a multiple-choice test item. Here are some guidelines for answering multiple-choice test items. Add information to each guideline as your teacher tells you more about it.

- Read the stem and underline key words such as *not, except, incorrect, false.* These words give you clues to the correct answer.

- Read the stem with each possible answer choice to decide which answer choice is correct.

- As you decide an answer choice is incorrect, draw a line through it.

- If there is one answer choice left, it is the answer you should select.

- If there is more than one answer choice left, reread each with the stem and choose the best answer.

- Do not change your answer unless you are sure it is incorrect.

- Answer all items unless there is a penalty for guessing.

Practice Taking a Multiple-Choice Test **6-6**

Take the following multiple-choice test. Apply the guidelines you learned for answering multiple-choice test items. There is no penalty for guessing. Each correct answer is worth one point. You have five minutes to complete the test.

Directions Circle the letter in front of the best answer for each of the following five items. Then wait for your teacher's directions.

1. Do not answer questions for which you are unsure of the answer when:
   a. you are running out of time.
   b. a question is difficult.
   c. there is a guessing penalty.
   d. you don't like the question.

2. You should ____________ an answer choice when you decide it is incorrect.
   a. choose
   b. reread
   c. rewrite
   d. draw a line through

3. You should ____________ key words in a stem.
   a. underline
   b. ignore
   c. cross out
   d. look up

4. Change your answer when it is:
   a. too long.
   b. correct.
   c. incorrect.
   d. too short.

5. Read the ____________ with each answer choice to decide which answer is correct.
   a. first word of a question
   b. last word of a question
   c. stem
   d. key word

Number Correct ____________
5 = Excellent
4 = Good
0–3 = Reread the information on 6-4 and 6-5

Guidelines for Taking True/False Tests 6-7

Here are some things you should do to improve your score on a true/false test. Add information to each guideline as your teacher tells you more about it.

- Choose TRUE unless you can prove that a statement is FALSE.

- For a statement to be TRUE, all parts of the statement must be true. For example, the statement below is FALSE because not all parts of it are true.

  All mammals have hair, are warm blooded, and can talk. True False

  This answer is FALSE because, although all mammals have hair and are warm blooded, not all mammals can talk.

- Be careful when reading statements that contain negatives such as *not, don't,* or *in* (*infrequent*) and *un* (*unfriendly*). A negative can completely change the meaning of a statement. For example:

1. Jane is going to the party.	1. He comes to school frequently.
2. Jane is not going to the party.	2. He comes to school infrequently.

- If a statement has two negatives in it, get rid of both negatives. This makes the statement much easier to understand. For example, look at the two statements that follow. The second one is easier to understand because the two negatives have been taken out.
  1. You cannot get good grades if you do not study.
  2. You can get good grades if you do study.

- Absolute statements are usually FALSE. Qualified statements are usually TRUE. For example, statement 1 is FALSE and statement 2 is TRUE.
  1. *All* people like to go to the movies on Friday.
  2. *Some* people like to go to the movies on Friday.

- If you are uncertain about an item, take a guess at the answer unless there is a penalty for guessing.

Practice Taking a True/False Test **6-8**

Take the following true/false test. Apply the guidelines you learned for answering true/false test items. There is no penalty for guessing. Each correct answer is worth one point. You have five minutes to complete the test.

Directions Circle TRUE or FALSE for each of the following seven items. Then wait for your teacher's directions.

TRUE FALSE 1. If a statement has two negatives, you should get rid of one of the negatives to make the statement easier to understand.

TRUE FALSE 2. Absolute statements are usually false.

TRUE FALSE 3. If any part of a statement is true, then the statement is true.

TRUE FALSE 4. If you cannot prove a statement is false, you should consider it to be true.

TRUE FALSE 5. A negative can completely change the meaning of a statement.

TRUE FALSE 6. If you are uncertain about an answer, guess even if there is a guessing penalty.

TRUE FALSE 7. Qualified statements are usually false.

Number Correct ____________

Grading Scale
7 = Excellent
6 = Good
0–5 = Reread the information on 6-8.

Guidelines for Taking Matching Tests **6-9**

Read the directions for the following matching test. Notice that the directions tell you how to match items in the first column with items in the second column. The matching test has been completed to show you how the matches are made.

Directions Find the things that go together. In front of each word in the second column, write the number of the word that goes with it from the first column.

1. turkey	4	4th of July
2. Santa Claus	1	Thanksgiving
3. U.S. flag	2	Christmas
4. firecracker	3	Memorial Day

Here are some things you should do to improve your score on matching tests. If you follow these guidelines, you will have a better chance of making correct matches. Add information to each guideline as your teacher tells you more about it.

- Read all the items in both columns before making any matches. In the example, you might have matched *U.S. flag* with *4th of July* if you had not read all the way down to *firecracker*.

- Start by making the easiest matches.

- Make all correct matches before guessing at any matches.

- Cross out items in both columns as you make matches.

- Make your best guess for any remaining matches unless there is a penalty for guessing.

Practice Taking Matching Tests 6-10

Here are two matching tests. Follow the guidelines you learned for taking matching tests to complete them. You have five minutes to complete the two tests. Each correct match is worth one point. There is no penalty for guessing.

Directions for Test One Match the sport terms in the first column with the sports in the second column. Write the number of the item in the first column on the line next to the item it goes with in the second column.

1. home run	____	football
2. foul shot	____	baseball
3. touchdown	____	basketball
4. birdie	____	tennis
5. serve	____	golf

Sometimes you will be asked to match items in the second column with items in the first column, as in the following.

Directions for Test Two Write the number of the item in the second column on the line next to the item it goes with in the first column. Then wait for your teacher's directions.

____	physician	1. product
____	broadcaster	2. airplane
____	pilot	3. prescription
____	salesperson	4. lesson
____	teacher	5. news

Total Number Correct ____________

Grading Scale

9–10 = Excellent

7–8 = Good

0–6 = Review the information on 6-10.

Guidelines for Taking Completion Tests **6-11**

A completion test item consists of a statement with part of the statement missing. The missing part is shown by a blank line. The missing part can be anywhere in the statement, and it can be one word or more than one word. Your job is to write in the missing part. Here are examples of completion items with the missing part in different places.

1. The Bill of Rights states your ______________________ as a citizen of the United States.
2. The capital of the state of California is ______________________ .
3. ______________________ is the current president of the United States.

Here are some things you can do to improve your score on a completion test. By following these guidelines you will have a better chance of completing items correctly. Add information to each guideline as your teacher tells you more about it.

- Read the statement and think about what is missing.

- Write an answer that logically completes the statement.

- Be sure your answer fits the statement grammatically.

- Use the length of the blank line as a clue to the length of the answer unless the length of the blank line is the same for every item in the test.

- Reread the statement with your answer in it to be sure it makes sense.

Practice Taking a Completion Test

Here is an example of a completion test. Follow the guidelines you just learned as you take this test. You will have five minutes to take the test. Each correct completion is worth one point. There is no penalty for guessing.

Directions Complete each statement by writing the missing part on the line. Then wait for your teacher's directions.

1. Too much sun can cause ____________________ .

2. The president of the United States is ____________________ .

3. ____________________ live in igloos at the north pole.

4. Milk is ____________________ in color.

5. Your ____________________ supply oxygen to your heart and brain.

6. The more you study, the ____________________ your grades will be.

7. ____________________ has the largest population of any country in the world.

8. The four seasons of the year are ____ .

Number Correct ______________

Grading Scale

7–8 = Excellent

5–6 = Good

0–4 = Review the information on 6-12.

Understanding Direction Words in Essay Tests

6-13

In an essay test you must write an answer to a question or statement. Sometimes your answer will be very long and sometimes just a few words. The key to writing a good answer is understanding the *direction word* in the question or statement. A **direction word** tells you what you have to do when writing an answer. Many of the direction words you find in essay test items mean the same thing. Here are the common direction words used by teachers when they write essay test items:

discuss, describe, explain

These three direction words have the same meaning. When you see them in an essay test item, they are telling you to write as much as you can about the topic in the item. For example,

Discuss the characteristics of good study habits.
Describe the characteristics of good study habits.
Explain the characteristics of good study habits.

diagram, illustrate

These two direction words tell you to make a drawing and to label each part.

Diagram how electricity flows through a light bulb.
Illustrate how electricity flows through a light bulb.

compare, contrast

To *compare* means to tell how two or more things are alike as well as how they are different. To *contrast* means to tell only how they are different.

Compare the system of government in the United States and China.

To answer this item, you must tell how these two systems are alike and how they are different.

Contrast the system of government in the United States and China.

To answer this item, you must tell only how the two systems are different.

list, outline

To *list* means to present information in some order. Each item is usually numbered. To *outline* means to give the main points. An outline usually contains numbers and letters. An outline is more detailed than a list.

List the four seasons of the year.
1. winter
2. spring
3. summer
4. fall

Prepare an **outline** showing the characteristics of the four seasons of the year.

A. winter
 1. cold
 2. snow
 3. ice

B. spring
 1. flowers
 2. rain

C. summer
 1. hot
 2. swimming
 3. sun

D. fall
 1. cool
 2. leaves fall

summarize

A *summary* is a short statement that tells something about all the important ideas.

Summarize what you have learned about each of the following direction words:

1. describe

____

2. diagram

____

3. compare

____

4. list

____

Guidelines for Taking Essay Tests **6-14**

There are a number of things you an do to write a good answer to an essay test item. Here are some guidelines for answering essay test items. Add information to each guideline as your teacher tells you more about it.

- Read and restate each item in your own words before attempting to answer it. In this way, you check to see if you understand the item.

- Decide if your answer needs to be long or just a few words. If your answer is going to be long, make a brief outline before writing your answer. This helps you organize your information.

- Answer all parts of the item.

- Write directly to the point of the item. This means that you must answer the question or statement and not write about something else you find interesting or happen to know about.

- Use pictures and diagrams to explain your ideas whenever you need to.

- Write neatly because teachers will not give you credit for something they cannot read.

- Proofread your answers for clarity, spelling, and grammar.

- When you are running out of time, quickly list the information you know about any remaining items so your teacher will see what you know. This may earn you some credit.

Practice Taking an Essay Test 6-15

Directions Answer the following essay test item. You have ten minutes to do so.

Explain the five things you should do when taking any test.

Chapter Six Mastery Assessment **6-16**

Directions Show what you have learned about preparing for and taking different types of tests by writing an answer for each of the following:

1. **Explain** the four things you should do to prepare for tests.

2. **List** the steps in the five-day study plan.

3. **Summarize** what you should do when taking each of the following types of tests:

   Multiple choice

   True/false

   Matching

   Completion

   Essay

ANSWERS FOR CHAPTER SIX REPRODUCIBLE ACTIVITIES

6-1 1. Find out what will be on the test. 2. Make sure your textbook notes are complete. 3. Make sure class notes are complete. 4. Begin preparing five days before the test.

6-2 Day 5. Read all notes and handouts and highlight important information.
Day 4. Use remembering strategies to remember this information.
Day 3. Rehearse information.
Day 2. Rehearse and write answers for questions you believe your teacher will ask.
Day 1. Rehearse before taking the test.

6-3 1. Read directions carefully. Ask your teacher to explain anything you do not understand. 2. Look at the entire test to see how much you have to do. 3. Decide how much time to use to answer each question. 4. Answer easier questions first. 5. Check your answers for correctness.

6-4 Answers will vary, but the format must match those shown on 6-4.

6-5 Notes will vary.

6-6 1. c. 2. d. 3. a. 4. c. 5. c.

6-7 Notes will vary.

6-8 1. False. 2. True. 3. False. 4. True. 5. True. 6. False. 7. False.

6-9 Notes will vary.

6-10 Test One
3 = football
1 = baseball
2 = basketball
5 = tennis
4 = golf
Test Two
3 = physician
5 = broadcaster
2 = pilot
1 = salesperson
4 = teacher

6-11 Notes will vary.

6-12 1. sun burn. 2. name of current president. 3. Eskimos. 4. white. 5. lungs. 6. better. 7. China. 8. summer, fall, winter, spring (seasons can be in any order).

6-13 1. Write as much as you can about something. 2. Make a drawing and label the parts. 3. To tell how something is alike and different. 4. Present information in an ordered way.

6-14 Notes will vary.

6-15 Answers will vary but should contain the essential information found on 6-3.

6-16 1. Same as for 6-1. 2. Same as for 6-2. 3. Multiple choice: Guidelines shown on 6-5. True/false: Guidelines shown on 6-7. Matching: Guidelines shown on 6-9. Completion: Guidelines shown on 6-11. Essay: Guidelines shown on 6-14.

CHAPTER 7

Solving Math Word Problems

CHAPTER OBJECTIVES

1. **Teach students about the SQRQCQ math word problem solving strategy.**
2. **Teach students to apply SQRQCQ to different types of math word problems.**

TITLES OF REPRODUCIBLE ACTIVITIES

7-1 Learning about SQRQCQ
7-2 Guided Use of SQRQCQ
7-3 More Guided Use of SQRQCQ
7-4 Identifying Important Information
7-5 Applying SQRQCQ
7-6 Using SQRQCQ to Solve a Percent Problem
7-7 Using SQRQCQ to Solve a Fraction Problem
7-8 Using SQRQCQ to Solve a Money Problem
7-9 Using SQRQCQ to Solve a Measurement Problem
7-10 Chapter Seven Mastery Assessment

SUGGESTIONS FOR USING THE REPRODUCIBLE ACTIVITIES

7-1 Learning about SQRQCQ

Introduce SQRQCQ as a strategy for solving math word problems. Explain that each letter stands for one of the steps in the strategy. Have students read about each step as you explain it. Then have students complete the activity.

7-2 Guided Use of SQRQCQ

Use this activity to review what each letter stands for in the mnemonic. Use the activity to demonstrate the use of SQRQCQ. Then have students answer the questions.

7-3 More Guided Use of SQRQCQ

Use this activity to provide a second demonstration of the use of SQRQCQ. Then have students answer the questions.

7-4 Identifying Important Information

Use this activity to help students differentiate between important and extraneous information in math word problems.

7-5 Applying SQRQCQ

Arrange students into learning pairs. Then have the pairs solve the math word problem using SQRQCQ.

7-6 Using SQRQCQ to Solve a Percent Problem
7-7 Using SQRQCQ to Solve a Fraction Problem
7-8 Using SQRQCQ to Solve a Money Problem
7-9 Using SQRQCQ to Solve a Measurement Problem

Use 7-6 through 7-9 to have students apply SQRQCQ to different types of math word problems.

7-10 Chapter Seven Mastery Assessment

Have students complete this assessment at any point you believe they have learned to use the SQRQCQ strategy. Review the results of the assessment with the students. Provide additional instruction as necessary.

Learning about SQRQCQ

7-1

SQRQCQ is a strategy you can use for working out and solving math word problems. Each of the letters stands for one of the six steps in the strategy. Read about each step as your teacher discusses it with you.

Survey	Read the entire word problem to learn what it is about. Ask your teacher to explain any terms or ideas you do not understand. Be sure you understand everything in the word problem before you go to the next step.
Question	Change the problem into a question. Sometimes it is helpful to read the problem out loud or to form a picture of the problem in your mind or to draw a picture of the problem. Doing these things will help you change the problem into a question. When you have changed the problem into a question, you are ready to go on to the next step.
Read	Read to find all the information you need to answer the question. Write the information down where you can see it. Check to be sure you have all the necessary information. Cross out or ignore information in the problem that is not needed to answer the question.
Question	Ask, "What computations must I do to answer the question?"
Compute	Set up the problem on paper and do the computations. Check your computations for accuracy. Circle your answer.
Question	Look at your answer, and ask: "Does my answer make sense?" Sometimes you will find that your answer simply could not be right because it does not fit with the facts in the problem. When this happens, go back through the steps of SQRQCQ until you arrive at an answer that does make sense.

Write the words for which each of these letters stands:

S

Q

R

Q

C

Q

Guided Use of SQRQCQ

7-2

Read this math word problem:

> This year 1,300 students attend Morrison School. Last year there were only 950 students. The school newspaper reported that next year there will be a 7% increase in the number of students attending Morrison School. The principal wants to know how many students will be attending Morrison School next year if the newspaper report is correct.

Here is how SQRQCQ is used to solve this math word problem.

Survey **Read the problem to find out what it is about.**
Ask your teacher to define or explain anything you do not understand. For example, you may need to ask what a "7% increase" means. From a survey of this problem, you learn that the principal wants to know how many students will attend Morrison School next year.

Question **Change the problem into a question.**
By changing the problem into a question, you will have a better idea of how to solve the problem. Sometimes reading the problem out loud, visualizing it, or drawing a picture will help you change the problem into a question. The question here is:

"How many students will attend Morrison School next year if there is a 7% increase?"

Read **Read the problem and write down the information you need to answer the question.**
Here is the information you need to write:

- The number of students attending Morrison School this year (1,300)
- The percentage by which this number is expected to increase next year (7%)

Cross out or ignore information you do not need. In this problem, you do not need to know the number of students who attended Morrison School last year. If you cross out or ignore this unnecessary information, it will not get in the way as you answer the question.

Question **Ask, "What computations must I do to answer the question?"**
In this problem you will need to multiply 1,300 by 7%. Then you must add this result to 1,300.

Compute **Do the computations on paper.**

1,300	1,300
× .07	+ .91
91.00	1,391

Be sure to check that you have done your computations correctly. Circle your answer.

Question **Ask, "Does my answer make sense?"**
Look at the question and decide if your answer makes sense. The answer 1,391 makes sense for this problem because you knew there would be more students at Morrison School next year. Your answer, 1,391, is more than the 1,300 students now attending Morrison School. If your answer was less than 1,300, you would know you had done something wrong. You would then have to go back through the steps in SQRQCQ to get the correct answer.

Answer these questions:

1. Why is it important to change a problem into a question?

2. Why is it a good idea to cross out or ignore information not needed to answer the question?

3. What should you do if you decide your answer does not make sense?

More Guided Use of SQRQCQ

7-3

Here is another math word problem for you to read and solve.

> Maria earns $45 a week working at the supermarket. She works 9 hours a week. She has been working at a supermarket for 6 months. She works 3 days a week. How much money does Maria earn an hour?

Here is how SQRQCQ is used to solve this math word problem.

Survey After reading this problem, you know that you must find out how much money Maria earns each hour she works.

Question You change the problem into a question:

"How much money an hour does Maria earn?"

Read You decide the following information is needed to answer the question:

- Earns $45 a week.
- Works 9 hours a week.

You decide the following information is not needed to answer the question:

- She has been working at a supermarket for 6 months.
- She works 3 days a week.

Question You decide that you will need to divide $45 by 9 hours to know how much money Maria earns an hour.

Compute You do the computation.

($5) an hour
9√45

Question You decide your answer makes sense. You know that your answer must be more than $1 an hour and less than $45 an hour.

Answer these questions:

1. Was there anything in the problem you did not understand?

2. If yes, what did you not understand?

3. Did you read the problem aloud, try to visualize it, or draw a picture to help you change the problem into a question?

4. What information was not needed to answer the question?

5. Write the six key words that help you remember the strategy for solving math word problems.

Identifying Important Information **7-4**

Here are some math word problems. Each has been changed into a question. Cross out any information in the problem you do not need to answer the question.

1. The city of Louisville is about 300 miles from Sam's home town of Ashley. Sam has lived in Ashley for 13 years. Sam drives to Louisville at a speed of 50 miles an hour. Sam's dad wants to know the number of hours it will take Sam to get to Louisville.

   How many hours will it take Sam to get from Ashley to Louisville?

2. Sal has hit 150 home runs during his baseball career. He has played baseball for 10 years and has been on 3 different teams. He expects to play baseball for 5 more years. Determine the average number of home runs Sal has hit each year.

   What is the average number of home runs Sal hit per year?

3. Jax is 14 years old today. In his home state he will be able to vote at 18 years of age. Jax wants to know how long it will be before he is able to vote.

   In how many years will Jax be able to vote?

4. Oxford has a population of 370,890. It has two airports, 6 hospitals, and 22 schools. Its sister city of Bowtown has a population of 78,987. Bowtown has fewer hospitals and schools and does not have an airport. Bowtown is only 13 miles from Oxford. Figure out the population difference between the two cities.

   How many more people live in Oxford than Bowtown?

Applying SQRQCQ

Work with your partner to solve the following math word problem using the SQRQCQ strategy.

In Hamilton there is an average of 32 inches of rain each year. A tree planted in Hamilton grew 3 inches the first year it was planted. It grew 7 inches the second year and 14 inches the third year. This tree will take almost 100 years to reach its full height. Find the average yearly growth rate for this tree.

S Tell what the problem is about.

Q Change the problem into a question.

R Write the information needed to answer the question. (Cross out any information not needed.)

Q Tell what computations you will use.

C Do the computations. Circle your answer. (Remember to check your computations.)

Q Does your answer make sense? Why?

Using SQRQCQ to Solve a Percent Problem

7-6

Solve the following math word problem by using SQRQCQ.

> There are 780 students and 46 teachers at John Martin School. The school secretary reported that 56% of the students are boys. The principal, Ms. Adams, wants to know the number of boys attending the school. She has been asked for this information by the president of the PTA.

S Tell what the problem is about.

Q Change the problem into a question.

R Write the information needed to answer the question. (Cross out any information not needed.)

Q Tell what computations you will use.

C Do the computations. Circle your answer. (Remember to check your computations.)

Q Does your answer make sense? Why?

Using SQRQCQ to Solve a Fraction Problem

7-7

Solve the following math word problem by using SQRQCQ.

Juan and Susan ordered a large pizza with extra cheese and pepperoni for an after school snack. A large pizza has 12 slices and costs $9.60. Juan said he had a big appetite and would eat $\frac{2}{3}$ of the pizza. Susan said that was fine but that Juan would then have to pay $\frac{2}{3}$ of the cost of the pizza. Juan wants to know what his cost will be.

S Tell what the problem is about.

Q Change the problem into a question.

R Write the information needed to answer the question. (Cross out any information not needed.)

Q Tell what computations you will use.

C Do the computations. Circle your answer. (Remember to check your computations.)

Q Does your answer make sense? Why?

Using SQRQCQ to Solve a Money Problem

7-8

Solve the following math word problem by using SQRQCQ.

Paula has been offered a job working after school each day at the Town Pharmacy. She would be paid $5 per hour for stacking shelves and waiting on customers. Paula's mother wants to know how much money Paula would be earning each week. Here is the schedule Paula would have to work:

Monday and Wednesday: 3:00–5:00
Tuesday and Thursday: 3:30–6:15
Friday: 5:15–7:45

S Tell what the problem is about.

Q Change the problem into a question.

R Write the information needed to answer the question. (Cross out any information not needed.)

Q Tell what computations you will use.

C Do the computations. Circle your answer. (Remember to check your computations.)

Q Does your answer make sense? Why?

Using SQRQCQ to Solve a Measurement Problem

7-9

Solve the following math problem by using SQRQCQ.

Marvin wants to build a cage for his pet rabbit. He wants to build the top and bottom out of wood and the sides of the cage from wire. The top and bottom each need to be 4 feet long and 3 feet wide. His sister needs to know the number of square feet of wood to buy at the lumber yard.

S Tell what the problem is about.

Q Change the problem into a question.

R Write the information needed to answer the question. (Cross out any information not needed.)

Q Tell what computations you will use.

C Do the computations. Circle your answer. (Remember to check your computations.)

Q Does your answer make sense? Why?

Chapter Seven Mastery Assessment **7-10**

Directions Show what you have learned about using SQRQCQ to solve math word problems.

1. The first step in SQRQCQ is **Survey.** What must you do n this step?

2. The second step in SQRQCQ is **Question.** What must you do to complete this step?

3. The third step in SQRQCQ is **Read.** What information must you identify when using this step?

4. The fourth step in SQRQCQ is **Question.** What question must you ask to complete this step?

5. The fifth step in SQRQCQ is **Compute.** What must you do in this step?

6. The sixth step in SQRQCQ is **Question.** What question must you ask to complete this step?

7. What should you do if your answer to the question in step 6 is NO?

ANSWERS FOR CHAPTER 7 REPRODUCIBLE ACTIVITIES

7-1 S = Survey. Q = Question. R = Read. Q = Question. C = Compute. Q = Question.

7-2 1. To understand what must be done to solve the problem. 2. So information not needed will not get in the way of answering the question. 3. Repeat the steps.

7-3 1–3. Answers will vary. 4. She has been working at a supermarket for 6 months. She works 3 days a week. 5. Survey, Question, Read, Question, Compute, Question.

7-4 Students should cross out "Sam has lived in Ashley for 13 years." 2. Cross out ". . . and has been on 3 different teams. He expects to play baseball for 5 more years." 3. Nothing needs to be crossed out. 4. Cross out "It has two airports, 6 hospitals, and 22 schools. Bowtown has fewer hospitals and schools and does not have an airport. Bowtown is only 13 miles from Oxford."

7-5 The average yearly growth rate for the tree. Q = What is the average yearly growth rate for the tree? R = Grew 3 inches the first year, 7 the second year, 14 the third year. Q = Add 3 + 7 + 14. Divide sum by 3. C = 8 inches average yearly growth. (Students should cross out "In Hamilton there is an average of 32 inches of rain each year. This tree will take almost 100 years to reach its full height."). Q = Yes. It is more than the first year's growth but less than the third year's growth.

7-6 S = The number of boys who attend John Martin School. Q = How many boys attend John Martin School? R = 780 students; 56% boys. (Students should cross out "The school secretary reported that . . . and 46 teachers. She has been asked for this information by the president of the PTA."). Q = Multiply 780 × 56%. Round to nearest whole number. C = 437 boys. Q = Yes. The number of boys is fewer than the number of students.

7-7 S = The amount Juan must pay for the pizza. Q = How much will the pizza cost Juan? R = Pizza cost $9.60. Juan will pay ⅔ of cost. (Students should cross out "Juan and Susan ordered a large pizza with extra cheese and pepperoni for an after school snack. Juan said he had a big appetite and would eat ⅔ of the pizza. Susan said that was fine but that . . . then".). Q = Divide $9.60 by ⅔. C = Juan's cost is $6.40. Q = Yes. Juan's cost was less than the cost of the whole pizza.

7-8 S = Money Paula will earn each week. Q = How much money will Paula earn each week? R = Is paid $5 an hour. Works Monday and Wednesday 3:00–5:00, Tuesday and Thursday 3:30–6:15, Friday 5:15–7:45. (Students should cross out "Paula has been offered a job working after school each day at the Town Pharmacy" and ". . . for stacking shelves and waiting on customers."). Q = Subtract ending from starting time for each day. Sum differences. Convert minutes to hours and minutes. C = $60 per week. Q = Yes. Paula works 2 to 3 hours per day for 5 days each week and is paid $5 an hour. This means the answer must be between $50 and $75 per week.

7-9 S = Number of square feet needed to build a wood top and bottom for a cage. Q = How many square feet of wood will Marvin's sister need to buy? R = Needs to build a wood top and bottom that are each 4 feet long and 3 feet wide. (Students should cross out ". . . for his pet rabbit . . . and the sides of the cage from wire."). Q = Multiply length × width × 2. C = 24 square feet of wood. Q = Yes. 12 square feet are needed for both the top and bottom of the cage.

7-10 1. Read the problem to learn what it is about. 2. Change the problem into a question. 3. The information needed to answer the question. 4. What computation(s) must I do? 5. (a) Set up the problem on paper. (b) Do the computation(s). (c) Check for accuracy. (d) Circle answer. 6. Does my answer make sense? 7. Repeat the steps to arrive at an answer that makes sense.

CHAPTER EIGHT

Using the Library

CHAPTER OBJECTIVES

1. **Teach students to use the library to find information.**
2. **Teach students to evaluate the sources of information they find.**

TITLES OF REPRODUCIBLE ACTIVITIES

8-1 A Strategy for Using the Library
8-2 Types of Materials Found in a Library
8-3 Learning about Card and Online Catalogs
8-4 Using a Card Catalog
8-5 Using an Online Catalog
8-6 Learning about the Dewey Decimal System
8-7 Locating Books by Call Number
8-8 Learning about Print and Electronic Indexes
8-9 Using CD ROM Databases
8-10 Using the Readers' Guide to Periodical Literature
8-11 Evaluating Sources of Information
8-12 Chapter Eight Mastery Assessment

SUGGESTIONS FOR USING THE REPRODUCIBLE ACTIVITIES

After you have distributed a reproducible activity, here are suggestions for its use. Feel free to add further information, illustrations, or examples. Wherever possible, relate the activity to actual subject area assignments.

8-1 A Strategy for Using the Library

Invite the librarian to your class. Ask the librarian to discuss with students how today's library contains information in both print and electronic form. Have the librarian guide students through the five steps and define any terms students do not know. Then have students answer the questions on their own.

8-2 Types of Materials Found in a Library

Describe each of the types of materials found in a library. Provide examples of each type where possible. Then have students complete the matching activity.

8-3 Learning about Card and Online Catalogs

Invite the librarian to your class. Ask the librarian to explain the difference between a card catalog and an online catalog. Have students ask the librarian any questions necessary to complete the activity.

8-4 Using a Card Catalog

If your library does not have a card catalog, do not use this activity.

Explain why there are three types of cards for each item. Describe the information that is on each card. Then have students answer the questions. Point out that all the subjects for the item can be found at the bottom of each type of card.

8-5 Using an Online Catalog

Review with the students the computer record from an online catalog. Point out that different online catalogs may arrange the information in different ways, but that all records contain the information shown for this record. Then have students answer the questions.

8-6 Learning about the Dewey Decimal System

Review the ten primary classes of the Dewey Decimal System with the students and have them complete the activity.

8-7 Locating Books by Call Number

Use the example to show students how call numbers in the Dewey Decimal System are arranged in numerical order. Review the concept of decimal points as necessary. Then have students complete the activity.

8-8 Learning about Print and Electronic Indexes

Explain to students that they need to use an index to identify articles in newspapers or magazines. These indexes may be in either print or electronic format. Point out that most school libraries have electronic indexes on CD ROM. Have students read about print and electronic indexes and answer the questions. Arrange a class with the school librarian to introduce students to the print indexes and CD ROM databases available in your library.

8-9 Using CD ROM Databases

Emphasize to students that a CD ROM database contains all the information needed to locate articles in magazines or newspapers. Point out that a CD ROM database contain abstracts of articles cited and sometimes entire articles as well. Have students examine the sample CD ROM record and answer the questions.

8-10 Using the *Readers' Guide to Periodical Literature*

Have students read the introductory text about the *Readers' Guide to Periodical Literature*. Review the parts of a citation in the example with the students. Explain the three steps to follow when using the *Readers' Guide*. Then direct students to complete the activity.

8-11 Evaluating Sources of Information

Lead students in a discussion about the sources from which they can obtain information in and out of the library. Have students write sources of information for the four places. Point out that some sources of information are more believable than others. Next, have students rate the believability of each source using the scale provided. Then have students compare their responses to see if some sources are more believable than others.

8-12 Chapter Eight Mastery Assessment

Have students complete this assessment at any point you believe they have learned how to find and evaluate information in the library. Review the results of the assessment with the students. Provide additional instruction as necessary.

A Strategy for Using the Library **8-1**

The library is a good place to find information. Librarians are there to help you find information. Most libraries also have computers you can use to find information. Here are the steps you should follow to find and use information in the library.

Step One:	Use the card catalog or online catalog to identify books and other sources of information located in the library.
Step Two:	Use print indexes and/or CD ROM databases to identify articles in magazines and newspapers.
Step Three:	Find books, articles in magazines and newspapers, and other sources of information on the library shelves.
Step Four:	Read and evaluate the information you find in these sources.
Step Five:	Use the information to do homework, prepare a written or oral report, or study for a test.

1. What would you use to identify books and other sources of information in the library?

2. What would you use to identify articles in magazines and newspapers?

3. What should you do with the information you find in sources of information?

4. What are three uses of the information?

Types of Materials Found in a Library **8-2**

You will find many different types of materials in a library. Read the names and descriptions of the types of materials found in the library. On the line in front of each name for a type of material, write the letter corresponding to its description.

Name

1. ______ book
2. ______ magazine
3. ______ audiocassette
4. ______ CD ROM
5. ______ microfiche
6. ______ reference book
7. ______ microfilm
8. ______ newspaper
9. ______ multimedia
10. ______ videocassette

Description

A. Flat plastic cards, usually 4″ × 6″, with small images of pages that can be read or copied on a special machine.
B. Materials to help you do research such as encyclopedias, almanacs, dictionaries, and indexes.
C. Cartridge containing a filmed or televised image, usually including sound, and viewed using a television monitor and VCR.
D. Small reel of plastic film that contains small images that can be read or copied on a special machine.
E. Small cartridge with recorded speech or sounds, and listened to using a tape recorder.
F. A daily publication containing news and opinions about current events, feature stories, and advertising.
G. Compact Disc Read Only Memory. A computer-based method of storing information as a database, requiring a computer and CD player for use.
H. Many pages written on a topic bound together in a single volume.
I. CD ROM database that includes text, video, sound, animation, color, and other features to provide information. Many reference books and encyclopedias are now available in this format.
J. A weekly or monthly publication, usually with glossy pictures and advertisements, containing articles on topics of general interest.

Learning about Card and Online Catalogs **8-3**

All libraries have a catalog listing materials found in the library. The catalog describes each item and tells where it is located. Some libraries have a card catalog where the information is typed on 3″ × 5″ cards and arranged alphabetically in file drawers. The file drawers are arranged in cabinets that look like this:

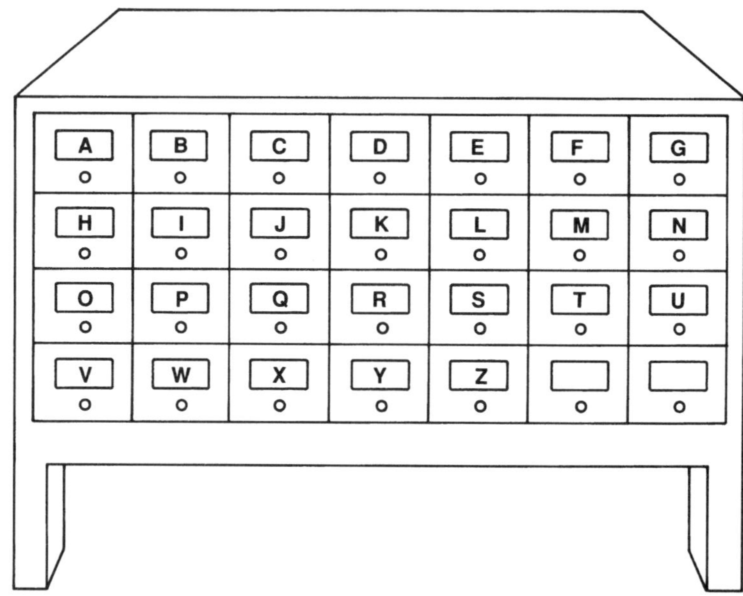

Use the information provided by your librarian to answer the questions.

1. Does your library have a card catalog? Yes No

2. If yes, circle each item you can find using your library's card catalog.

   books magazines videocassettes

   audiocassettes newspapers

3. Some libraries have an online catalog where the information is entered into a computer. Most libraries name their online catalogs. Does your library have an online catalog? Yes No

4. If yes, does your online catalog have a name? Yes No

   If yes, write its name here:

5. Some online catalogs provide connections to other libraries or to the Internet. Does your online catalog provide connections to information that is *not* located in your library?

   If yes, describe what you have learned about the online catalog in your library.

Using a Card Catalog

8-4

A card catalog lists all the items found in the library. Information about each item is typed on a card and the cards are filed alphabetically in drawers. Each item has three types of cards to allow you to look for items in three different ways: by subject, title, or author.

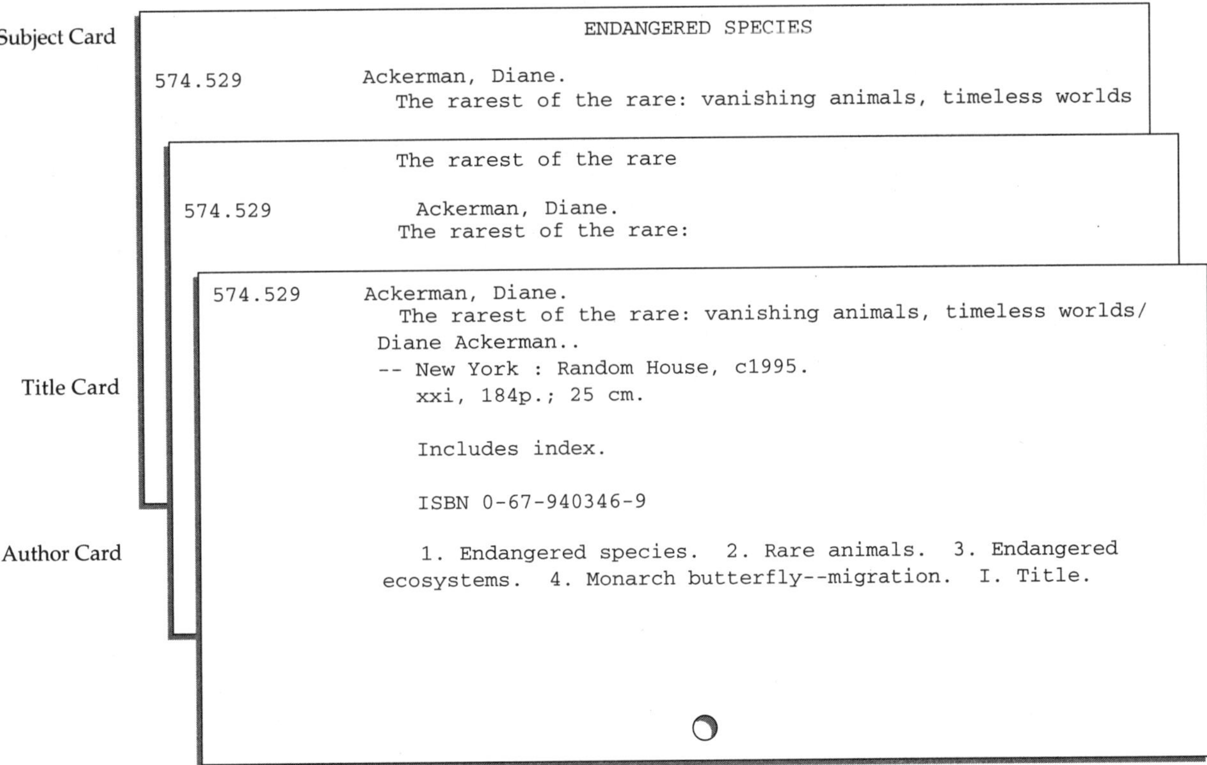

1. What is the title of this book?

2. Who wrote it?

3. Under what subjects would you look to find this book?

4. When was this book published?

5. Who is the publisher?

6. How many pages are there?

Using an Online Catalog **8-5**

Online catalogs include all of the information about each item the library owns. The information about each item is arranged on a computer record. Look at the computer record and answer the questions.

Author:	Willis, Jerry, W.
Title:	Technology, reading and language arts/ Jerry W. Willis, Elizabeth C. Stephens, Kathryn J. Matthew.
Imprint:	Boston: Allyn & Bacon, 1996
Call Number:	428.4
Physical features:	xix, 229p. : ill.; 24 cm.
Other authors:	Stephens, Elizabeth C.
	Matthew, Kathryn J.
Subjects:	Reading -- computer-assisted instruction
	Language arts -- computer-assisted instruction
	Educational technology

1. Under what subjects could you find this book?

2. What is its title?

3. Who wrote it?

4. In what year was it published?

5. Who is the publisher?

6. How many pages are there?

7. Does the book have any illustrations?

8. What is its call number?

Learning about the Dewey Decimal System

8-6

Most school libraries are organized using the Dewey Decimal System. Books on similar subjects are grouped together under ten primary classes. The ten primary classes are represented by numbers. Here are the ten primary classes and the numbers that go with each.

000–099	Generalities	500–599	Pure Science
100–199	Philosophy and Related Areas	600–699	Technology (Applied Sciences)
200–299	Religion	700–799	The Arts
300–399	The Social Sciences	800–899	Literature and Rhetoric
400–499	Language	900–999	General Geography, History, etc.

Under which numbers would you find books on the following topics:

1. the composer Mozart

2. physics in the atomic age

3. Protestant leaders

4. Spanish terms and expressions

5. a general encyclopedia

6. countries that make up South America

7. the Greek philosopher Aristotle

8. the writer Shakespeare

9. U.S. government

10. using robots in industry

Locating Books by Call Number **8-7**

A catalog in a library will give you the call number for a book. There are different systems of call numbers, but most school and public libraries use the Dewey Decimal System. The Dewey Decimal call number is a series of numbers with decimals typed on the spine of a book. The call number tells the subject of the book and where it can be found on the library shelves. You need to know how to arrange call numbers in numerical order to find books quickly on the library shelves.

Look at these books. Each book has its Dewey Decimal call number printed on its spine. The books have been placed in numerical order from left to right.

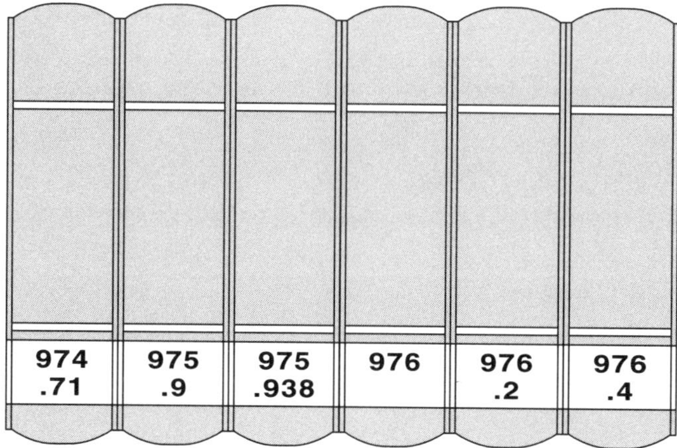

Here are more books with their Dewey Decimal call number. Write the numbers 1–6 under each book to show how these books would be arranged in numerical order.

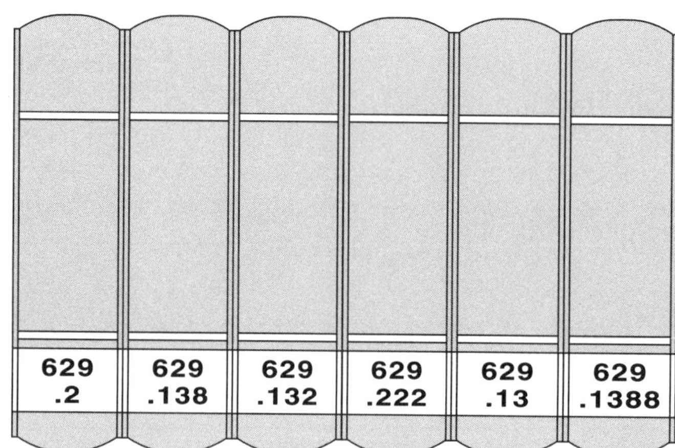

Learning about Print and Electronic Indexes

8-8

Indexes help you locate articles in thousands of different magazines or newspapers. Many school libraries own electronic indexes on CD ROM. A CD ROM index is also called a database. Many CD ROM databases contain an abstract for each article. An abstract is a short summary of the article. In some cases the entire article is also included. The entire article is called the full text.

1. What is another name for a CD ROM index?

2. Can you sometimes find the entire article?

3. What is the difference between an abstract and full text?

Libraries that do not have a CD ROM database will have print indexes. Print indexes look like books. You use them to look up your topic. You will find almost any topic in most indexes. Some indexes cover only one subject, like art or science.

4. Where do you look for magazine and newspaper articles if your library does not have a CD ROM database?

5. Can you find almost any topic in most indexes?

6. Are there indexes that cover topics in only one subject?

Using CD ROM Databases

8-9

CD ROM databases provide citations to articles about a topic. Each citation contains all the information needed to find the article. In addition, the CD ROM database includes the abstract of the article and sometimes also includes the full text. Information about the article is arranged in a record. There is one record for each article. Look at the sample record:

Sample CD ROM Record (from SIRS Researcher, SIRS, Inc. 1996)

Volume:	SIRS 1995 Population, Volume Number 4, Article 3	
Subject:	Keyword(s) : WATER and POLLUTION	
Title:	Earth Is Running Out of Room	
Author:	Lester R. Brown	
Source:	USA Today (Magazine)	
Publication Date:	Jan. 1995	Page Number(s): 30–32

Use the sample record to answer these questions:

1. What is the title of this article?

2. What magazine published this article?

3. When was the article published?

4. What is the name of the database used to locate this record?

5. What is the article about?

6. Who wrote the article?

7. How long is the article?

Using the Readers' Guide to Periodical Literature

8-10

The *Readers' Guide to Periodical Literature* is often called by its abbreviated name, the *Readers' Guide*. It is a print index to magazine articles. Use the *Readers' Guide* when you want to find magazine articles on your topic and your library does not have a CD ROM database. The *Readers' Guide* lists citations to articles. Each citation includes the information you need to find the article. Here is an example of a citation with its parts labeled.

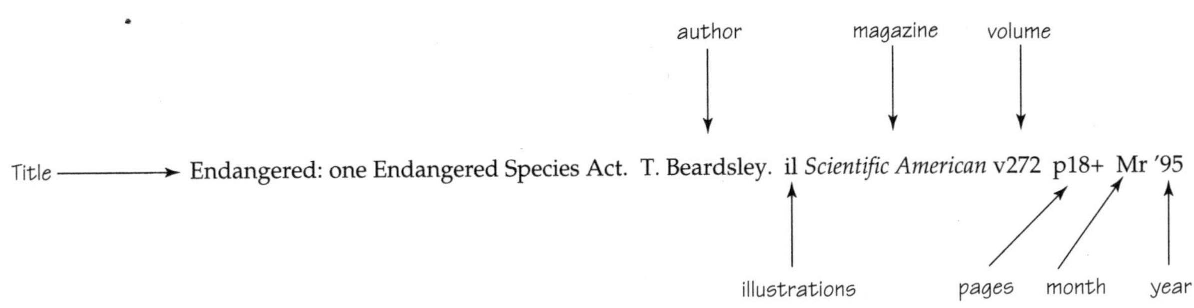

Follow these steps when using the *Readers' Guide* to locate information about a topic.

Step One.	Look up your topic in the current volume.
Step Two.	Identify citations related to the topic.
Step Three.	Check to see if the magazine in the citation is available in your library.

Here is another citation.

① ② ④ ⑤

Nature teaches us: it's hard to reweave the fabric of diversity. J.D. Hair. il *International Wildlife* v25 p26 My/Je '95

③ ⑥ ⑦ ⑧

Write the label for each part next to the numbers below:

1.

2.

3.

4.

5

6.

7.

8.

Evaluating Sources of Information 8-11

You can get information in many places. Each place has many sources of information. Think about sources of information for each of the following places. Write five sources of information for each place.

At the Library

1. ______________________ ( )
2. ______________________ ( )
3. ______________________ ( )
4. ______________________ ( )
5. ______________________ ( )

At School

1. ______________________ ( )
2. ______________________ ( )
3. ______________________ ( )
4. ______________________ ( )
5. ______________________ ( )

In the Car

1. ______________________ ( )
2. ______________________ ( )
3. ______________________ ( )
4. ______________________ ( )
5. ______________________ ( )

At Home

1. ______________________ ( )
2. ______________________ ( )
3. ______________________ ( )
4. ______________________ ( )
5. ______________________ ( )

Some sources of information are more **believable** than others. Evaluate the believability of each source you listed by rating each source on the following scale. Write your rating inside the ( ).

N = Not Believable
P = Possibly Believable
B = Believable

Chapter Eight Mastery Assessment **8-12**

See what you have learned about using the library to find information:

1. What are the five steps in the strategy for using the library?

2. What is multimedia?

3. What does a library catalog list?

4. What are the three different types of cards found in a card catalog?

5. How is the information about each item in an online catalog arranged?

6. How many primary classes does the Dewey Decimal System include?

7. What two things are told by a call number?

8. What is another name for a CD ROM index?

9. When should you use the *Readers' Guide?*

ANSWERS FOR CHAPTER EIGHT REPRODUCIBLE ACTIVITIES

8-1 1. Card catalog or online catalog.
2. Print indexes and/or CD ROM databases.
3. Read and evaluate it.
4. Do homework, prepare a report, study for a test.

8-2 1. H; 2. J; 3. E; 4. G; 5. A; 6. B; 7. D; 8. F; 9. I; 10. C.

8-3 Answers will vary.

8-4 1. The rarest of the rare: vanishing animals, timeless worlds. 2. Diane Ackerman. 3. Endangered species; Rare animals; Endangered ecosystems; Monarch butterfly--migration. 4. 1995. 5. Random House. 6. 184.

8-5 1. Reading--computer-assisted instruction; Language arts--computer-assisted instruction; Educational technology.
2. Technology, reading and language arts.
3. Jerry W. Willis, Elizabeth C. Stephens, Kathryn J. Matthew.
4. 1996. 5. Allyn & Bacon. 6. 229. 7. Yes. 8. 428.4

8-6 1. 700–799 2. 500–599 3. 200–299 4. 400–499 5. 000–099 6. 900–999 7. 100–199 8. 800–899 9. 300–399 10. 600–699

8-7 (5) (3) (2) (6) (1) (4)

8-8 1. CD ROM database. 2. Yes. 3. An abstract is a short summary of the article; full text is the entire article. 4. Print indexes. 5. Yes. 6. Yes.

8-9 1. Earth Is Running Out of Room. 2. USA Today. 3. Jan. 1995. 4. SIRS Researcher. 5. WATER and POLLUTION. 6. Lester R. Brown. 7. three pages.

8-10 1. title. 2. author. 3. illustrations. 4. magazine. 5. volume. 6. pages. 7. month. 8. year.

8-11 Answers will vary.

8-12 1. Step 1. Use the card catalog or online catalog to identify books and other sources of information located in the library. Step 2. Use print indexes and/or CD ROM databases to identify articles in magazines and newspapers. Step 3. Find books, articles in magazines and newspapers, and other sources of information on the library shelves. Step 4. Read and evaluate the information you find in these sources. Step 5. Use the information to do homework, prepare a written or oral report, or study for a test.
2. CD ROM database that includes text, video, sound, animation, color, and other features to provide information.
3. Materials found in the library.
4. Subject card; title card; author card.
5. On a record.
6. Ten.
7. Subject of a book; where it can be found on the shelf.
8. CD ROM database.
9. When library does not have a CD ROM database.

CHAPTER NINE

Using the Internet

CHAPTER OBJECTIVES

1. **Teach students to use the Internet to find information.**
2. **Teach students to evaluate the sources of information they find.**

TITLES OF REPRODUCIBLE ACTIVITIES

9-1 Learning about the Internet
9-2 A Strategy for Using the Internet
9-3 Using the World Wide Web
9-4 Another Web Page
9-5 Learning about E-mail
9-6 Learning about Your Local FreeNet
9-7 Sightseeing on the Internet
9-8 Evaluating Sources of Information on the Internet
9-9 Chapter Nine Mastery Assessment

SUGGESTIONS FOR USING THE REPRODUCIBLE ACTIVITIES

After you have distributed a reproducible activity, here are some suggestions for its use. Feel free to add further information, illustrations or examples. Wherever possible, relate the activity to actual subject area assignments.

9-1 Learning about the Internet

Review the introductory text describing the Internet. Clarify terms and concepts as necessary. Have students answer questions 1 and 2. Next, review the text about Internet services. Have students answer questions 3–7.

9-2 A Strategy for Using the Internet

You may do this activity yourself, or invite the school librarian to your class. Explain that, in addition to the library, the Internet is another source for information. Guide students through the four steps of the strategy for using the Internet. Then have students answer the questions. For Step Three, emphasize that because anyone can put information on the Internet, evaluating information found on the Internet is especially important.

9-3 Using the World Wide Web

Go over the introductory text with the students. Note that the sample page provided is a home page because it is the top page in a set of pages by the Department of the Treasury. Review the information on the Department of the Treasury home page. Have students answer the questions about the Department of the Treasury home page. Encourage students to bring in examples of other web pages to share with the class. Point out that web pages vary considerably.

9-4 Another Web Page

Have the students look at the home page for the White House and answer the questions. Lead a discussion about how this page is different from the Department of the Treasury page.

9-5 Learning about E-mail

Review the introductory text describing e-mail. Have students answer the questions. Then lead a discussion about using e-mail to "talk" to other students around the world. Have students answer the remaining questions. Finally, ask students to share their responses.

9-6 Learning about Your Local FreeNet

Use this activity only if your community has a FreeNet. Check with your public library if you are uncertain whether there is one.

Review the introductory text with your students. Have the students look at the choices on the sample FreeNet menu. Direct the students to complete the activity. You can vary this activity by using a menu from your own local FreeNet.

9-7 Sightseeing on the Internet

Use this activity only if your school provides access to the World Wide Web with a graphical interface. (such as Netscape Navigator or Internet Explorer or NCSA Mosaic)

Review the list of Internet sites provided. Describe to students any of these places they may not know. Then direct students to select a place to "visit." Explain that the World Wide Web will allow them to see pictures. Help students connect to and search the sites they selected. If you have problems connecting, or if the web address has changed, select another site from the list provided. Then direct students to answer the questions about the site they selected.

9-8 Evaluating Sources of Information on the Internet

Use this activity only if your school provides access to the World Wide Web.

Explain to students that anyone can put information on the Internet. Emphasize the importance of evaluating the source of the information found on the Internet.

Provide students with possible sites to visit and help them to connect to and search these sites. Take students through the five steps for learning about the source of information found at the site they visit. Then have students evaluate the believability of the source of information they found.

9-9 Chapter Nine Mastery Assessment

Have students complete this assessment at any point you believe they have learned how to find information using the Internet. Review the results of the assessment with the students. Provide additional instruction as necessary.

Learning about the Internet

9-1

The **Internet** is a worldwide network of computers and the cables that connect them. It is often called the **information superhighway** because it is like a network of roads that you can travel to get from your computer to other computers around the world.

1. What is the Internet?

2. Why is the Internet called the information superhighway?

The **World Wide Web** (WWW) and **e-mail** (electronic mail) are two services you can use on the Internet. You can use the WWW to find information. You can use e-mail to send messages to and receive messages from anyone around the world who has a connection to the Internet.

3. What two services can you use on the Internet?

4. Why would you use the World Wide Web?

5. Why would you use e-mail?

6. What does WWW stand for?

7. What does e-mail stand for?

A Strategy for Using the Internet **9-2**

The Internet is a good place to look for information. You can use the Internet in your classroom, your library, or at home. Your teacher can tell you if the Internet is available in your school. Here are the steps you should follow to find and use information on the Internet.

Step One: Use the World Wide Web to find information on the Internet.
Step Two: Identify the source of the information. Common sources include governments, private organizations, companies, or individuals.
Step Three: Read and evaluate the information you find on the Internet.
Step Four: Use the information to do homework, prepare a written or oral report, or study for a test.

1. What would you use to find information on the Internet?

2. What are common sources of information on the Internet?

3. What should you do with the information after you find it?

4. What are three uses for the information?

Using the World Wide Web 9-3

The **World Wide Web** (WWW) is the most popular way to explore the Internet. Information on the WWW is organized on **web pages**. The first or top page in a set of web pages is called the **home page**. When you use the WWW to find information, you can click on a highlighted ("hot") word, phrase, or image on a web page to jump to another place where you will find information related to that word, phrase, or image. Here is an example of a web page.
Refer to the sample home page to answer the following questions:

Text Only Version

Browse / What's New / Who's Who / Treasury Offices / Tours & Treasures / Correspondence /
Search / Email Web Master / Treasury Mission

The Treasury World Wide Web Site was last updated on Monday, March 17, 1997.

1. What is the name of the home page?

2. On the computer screen, hot words or phrases are highlighted in different colors from the rest of the text. These "hot" words or phrases are underlined when printed. Write at least three hot words or phrases found on this page.

3. The bottom of a page often provides information about the page itself: the source of the information, the number of visitors, when it was last updated, an e-mail address, and so on. When was this web site last updated?

4. Can you send e-mail from this web page? to whom?

Another Web Page

9-4

Web pages are very different from one another. Some are easy to use, whereas others are confusing. Some are useful; others are inaccurate and misleading. Some are educational, others are just for fun. Here is another example of a web page.

Refer to the sample web page to answer the following questions.

1. What is the name of the web page?

2. Can you tell what organization is responsible for the information on this web page?

3. Some web pages have navigation buttons that you can click on to jump to another page of information. "White House History and Tours" is one of the navigation buttons on the sample page. Write the name of another navigation button found on this page.

4. Which navigation button would you press to send e-mail to the president?

5. Which button would you press to obtain statistics about the government?

6. Which button would you press to find out about activities for children?

Learning about E-mail **9-5**

You can use e-mail (electronic mail) to send messages to and receive messages from anyone around the world who has a connection to the Internet. You must turn on your computer to send an e-mail message. However, you can receive e-mail in your mailbox even when your computer is turned off.

When you turn on your computer and open your mailbox, you will find any new messages that have been sent to you. Here are some of the things you can do with a message:

Read—read the message.
Delete—erase the message.
Forward—send the message to another electronic mailbox.
Reply—answer the person who wrote you the message.
Print—print the message.

1. Can you send e-mail when your computer is turned off?

2. Can you receive e-mail when your computer is turned off?

3. What are five things you can do with e-mail messages?

You can use e-mail to "talk" to students in other schools all over the world. Think of some reasons you might want to talk to a student in another state or country. Then answer the following questions.

4. What place in the world would you pick to send an e-mail message to another student?

5. Why did you pick this place?

6. What would you want to talk about?

Learning about Your Local FreeNet **9-6**

A FreeNet has information about a particular community. There are FreeNets in many cities, towns, and rural areas throughout the world. There may be one for your community. FreeNets provide a free connection to the Internet. You can also use a FreeNet to send and receive e-mail.

Information on a FreeNet is usually arranged in menus like the one that follows.

```
SEFLIN FREE-NET - DADE COUNTY EDITION
 1. About SEFLIN Free-Net (Administration)        (admin)
 2. Around the Network (INDEX)                    (index)
 3. Arts & Entertainment District                 (arts)
 4. Business & Industrial Park                    (business)
 5. Comm Central (Mailbox,Teleport,Newsstand)     (cc)
 6. Education Center                              (school)
 7. Government & Communities Information Complex  (govern)
 8. Home, Garden, & Daily Living                  (home)
 9. Legal, Financial & Tax Building               (legal)
10. Library & Literary Complex                    (library)
11. Medical & Health Center                       (health)
12. Religion & Philosophy Center                  (religion)
13. Science & Technology Center                   (science)
14. Social Services Complex                       (social)
15. Special Interest Groups                       (special)
16. Sports Arena & Recreation Center              (sports)
17. Youth Center                                  (teen)
```

Source: South East Florida Library Information Network. FreeNet. Dade County Edition.

Refer to the sample FreeNet menu. What number would you select for each of the following? Write the number on the line provided.

1. ____ Find out about local fairs and festivals.

2. ____ Find out about a local sports team.

3. ____ Find information for a science fair.

4. ____ Use e-mail.

5. ____ Connect to library online catalogs.

6. ____ Find out what the mayor of your community is planning.

7. ____ Learn how to plant a tree.

8. ____ Find out about safe ways to exercise for health.

Sightseeing on the Internet 9-7

The World Wide Web allows you to travel around the world on the information superhighway. You can stop to visit places of interest. Here is a list of tourist attractions, museums, and other places you might want to visit. Next to each place is its web address.

Metropolitan Museum of Art	http://www.metmuseum.org
Disneyworld	http://www.disney.com
NASA/Kennedy Space Station	http://www.ksc.nasa.gov/ksc.html
Louvre	http://www.paris.org/Musees/Louvre/info.html
Buckingham Palace	http://www.u-net.com/hotelnet/palace/home.htm
Smithsonian Museum	http://www.si.edu
Alcatraz	http://www.nps.gov/alcatraz
Sistine Chapel	http://www.christusrex.org/www1/sistine/0-Tour.html

Select one of these places and visit it on the World Wide Web. Then answer the following questions about the place you visited.

1. What is the name of one navigation button on the home page?

2. What is one "hot" word or phrase on the home page?

3. Describe the picture you liked best at the place you visited.

4. What are three things you learned about the place you visited?

Evaluating Sources of Information on the Internet 9-8

Anyone can make information available on the Internet. It is up to you to decide if the information is believable. To evaluate the believability of the information you find on the Internet, you must learn about the source of the information. Here are five steps you can follow to learn about the source of information you find on the Internet.

Step One Locate a web page on the Internet. Write down the URL for the site where you located the information. The URL (uniform resource locator) is the "address" where you found the information. It usually starts with:

http:// ____

Step Two Look at your URL to see if it has any of the following parts. These parts tell something about the source of the information. Circle a part if your URL contains it.

.com = commercial .gov = government . edu = education .org = organization

Step Three Look at the top of the home page. Is there anything that identifies the creator of the information such as the name of a company, person, or organization? If provided, write information about the creator here.

Step Four Look at the bottom of the page to see if there is anything that identifies the creator. If provided, write information about the creator here.

Step Five Look at the bottom of the page. It might say "this page maintained by . . ." or provide the name of an "author" or "creator." It may also provide an e-mail address or a button to send e-mail. What information about the source is provided at the bottom of your page?

Some sources of information are more believable than others. Is the source of information for your web page (check ✓ one) ________ believable ________ possibly believable ________ not believable. Why?

Chapter Nine Mastery Assessment

9-9

See what you have learned about using the Internet to find information:

1. What is the Internet?

2. What are common sources of information on the Internet?

3. What is a home page?

4. What is a navigation button?

5. What can you do with e-mail?

6. What is a URL?

7. Who can make information available on the Internet?

8. Why is it important to learn about the source of information found on the Internet?

ANSWERS FOR CHAPTER NINE REPRODUCIBLE ACTIVITIES

9-1 1. Worldwide network of computers and the cables that connect them. 2. Because it is like a network of roads that you can travel to get from your computer to other computers around the world. 3. World Wide Web and e-mail. 4. To find information. 5. To send messages to and receive messages from anyone around the world who has a connection to the Internet. 6. World Wide Web. 7. Electronic mail.

9-2 1. World Wide Web. 2. Governments, private organizations, companies, or individuals. 3. Read and evaluate it. 4. Do homework, prepare a written or oral report, study for a test.

9-3 1. Welcome to the Department of the Treasury. 2. Browse; What's New; Who's Who; Treasury Offices; Search. 3. March 12, 1997. 4. Yes. To the Web Master.

9-4 1. Welcome to the White House. 2. No. 3. The president & vice-president; Interactive Citizens' Handbook; The Virtual Library; White House Help Desk; What's New; White House History and Tours; Commonly Requested Federal services; Site News; The Briefing Room; or White House for Kids. 4. The president & Vice-President. 5. The Briefing Room. 6. White House for Kids.

9-5 1. No. 2. Yes. 3. Read, Delete, Forward, Reply, Print. 4. Answers will vary. 5. Answers will vary. 6. Answers will vary.

9-6 1. 3. 2. 16. 3. 13. 4. 5. 5. 10. 6. 7. 7. 8. 8. 11.

9-7 Answers will vary.

9-8 Answers will vary.

9-9 1. World wide network of computers and the cables that connect them. 2. Governments, private organizations, companies, or individuals. 3. The first or top page in a set of web pages. 4. Button on a web page that you can click on to jump to another page of information. 5. Send messages to and receive messages from anyone around the world who has a connection to the Internet. 6. The URL (uniform resource locator) is the address where you find information on the World Wide Web. 7. Anyone. 8. To help decide if the information is believable.

CHAPTER TEN

Using Reference Sources

CHAPTER OBJECTIVES

1. **Teach students about reference sources available in both print and electronic form.**
2. **Teach students how to locate and use basic reference sources.**

TITLES OF REPRODUCIBLE ACTIVITIES

10-1 Identifying and Locating Reference Sources
10-2 Print and Electronic Dictionaries
10-3 Information Found on a Dictionary Page
10-4 Putting Words in Alphabetical Order
10-5 Using Guide Words in a Dictionary
10-6 Phonetic Respellings in a Dictionary
10-7 Choosing the Correct Definition
10-8 Learning about Print and Electronic Encyclopedias
10-9 Using Print and Electronic Encyclopedias
10-10 Understanding an Encyclopedia Index Entry
10-11 Using a Thesaurus
10-12 Practice Using Synonyms
10-13 Using an Almanac
10-14 Using an Atlas
10-15 Using Biographical Sources of Information
10-16 Chapter Ten Mastery Assessment

SUGGESTIONS FOR USING THE REPRODUCIBLE ACTIVITIES

After you have distributed a reproducible activity, here are suggestions for its use. Feel free to add further information, illustrations, or examples. Wherever possible, relate the activity to actual subject area assignments.

10-1 Identifying and Locating Reference Sources

Use the introductory text to discuss frequently used types of reference sources. Show examples of these reference sources. Point out that reference sources are available in both print and electronic formats. Then have students answer the questions.

You may want to invite the school librarian to introduce your students to the reference sources available in the school library. This could be done at the library or in your classroom.

10-2 Print and Electronic Dictionaries

Review the introductory text with students. Have students read about unabridged and abridged dictionaries, and electronic dictionaries. Show students an example of each type of dictionary. Then have students answer the questions.

10-3 Information Found on a Dictionary Page

Have students read the descriptions of the different types of information found on a dictionary page. Have students complete the activity. Then ask students to look at a page in a dictionary they use to see if all the types of information are included. Refer students to the library if they do not own a dictionary.

10-4 Putting Words in Alphabetical Order

Explain that entry words are listed in alphabetical order so they can be found easily. Have students complete the activity.

10-5 Using Guide Words in a Dictionary

Show students an example of guide words from a dictionary you have in your classroom. Explain how opening and closing guide words are used to find entry words in a dictionary quickly. Point out to students that they do not have to know the meanings of the guide words. Have students complete the activity.

10-6 Phonetic Respellings in a Dictionary

Review the introductory text with students. Have students use a dictionary to complete the activity. Then have students volunteer to pronounce the words using the phonetic respellings.

10-7 Choosing the Correct Definition

Point out that dictionaries show more than one definition of a word arranged in order of how frequently each definition is used. Explain to students that when they choose a definition, they must consider the context in which the word is used. Then have students complete the activity.

10-8 Learning about Print and Electronic Encyclopedias

Review the introductory text with students. Have students read about the four types of encyclopedias. Show students any encyclopedias you have in your classroom and have them identify the type for each. Then have students answer the questions. Show electronic encyclopedias, if available.

10-9 Using Print and Electronic Encyclopedias

Have students use a library to complete the activity. Remind students to ask the librarian for assistance if they cannot find one or more of the types of encyclopedias.

10-10 Understanding an Encyclopedia Index Entry

Tell students they should use the index of an encyclopedia to locate information about a topic. Point out that the volume in which they might expect to find the topic may not contain the topic or may not contain all the information about the topic. For example, a student looking for information about hexagons might not find "Hexagon" as the title of an article in the "H" volume. However, the student might find an entry for "hexagon" in the index, with the direction to look under "polygons," found in the "P" volume.

Discuss the different types of information found in an encyclopedia index entry. Then have students look at the sample entry for "endangered species" and answer the questions.

10-11 Using a Thesaurus

Review the introductory text with students. Have students use a thesaurus to complete the activity.

10-12 Practice Using Synonyms

Use the example to show students how the meaning of a sentence can be changed by substituting a synonym for one of the words. Have students complete the activity.

10-13 Using an Almanac

Review the introductory text with students. Tell them they should use the index to find information in an almanac. Caution students that depending on the almanac they use, the index may be in the front, middle, or back. Have students locate almanacs in the library to complete the activity. You can use this activity as a group project or as a competition between individuals and/or groups. Later, lead a discussion about the way students located information and what they learned about using almanacs.

10-14 Using an Atlas

Review the introductory text with students. Emphasize that students may have to use more than one atlas to answer a question. Have students locate atlases to complete the activity. You can use this activity as a group project or as a competition between individuals and/or groups. Later, lead a discussion about the way students located information and what they learned about using atlases.

10-15 Using Biographical Sources of Information

Review the word *biography* with students. Tell them that they can find information about a person in an encyclopedia, but that biographical sources often provide more information than encyclopedias. Also point out that biographical sources contain information about people who do not appear in encyclopedias. Then have students locate biographical sources in the library to complete the activity.

10-16 Chapter Ten Mastery Assessment

Have students complete this assessment at any point you believe they have learned about print and electronic forms of reference sources and how to locate and use them. Review the results of the assessment with the students. Provide additional instruction as necessary.

Identifying and Locating Reference Sources

10-1

Reference sources are used to find background information on a topic, to find facts, and to get a quick answer to a question.

The most frequently used types of reference sources are dictionaries, encyclopedias, thesauruses, almanacs, and atlases. Reference sources are usually shelved in their own section of the library. You should ask the librarian to help you locate and use reference sources.

1. What are three uses of reference sources?

2. What are the five most frequently used types of reference sources?

3. Who can help you locate and use reference sources?

4. What reference sources have you used in the past?

Many reference sources are available on CD ROM. Some CD ROM reference sources are *multimedia*. They are called multimedia because they contain images, sound, video, and animation. Other CD ROM reference sources are *text-only*. This means they do not include images, sound, video, and animation.

5. What do multimedia reference sources contain?

6. What are text-only CD ROM reference sources?

Print and Electronic Dictionaries 10-2

Dictionaries are reference books that provide information about words. Dictionaries provide information about the meaning, pronunciation, and spelling of words. They are available in print and electronic form. Two important types of dictionaries you should know about are unabridged dictionaries and abridged dictionaries.

Unabridged Dictionaries

Unabridged dictionaries attempt to include all words currently in use in a language. They are usually very large. An example of an unabridged dictionary is the *Random House Dictionary of the English Language.*

Abridged Dictionaries

Abridged dictionaries omit words that are not frequently used. They are smaller, lighter, and less expensive than unabridged dictionaries. An example of an abridged dictionary is the *American Heritage Dictionary.*

1. What type of dictionary includes almost every word that people use today?
2. What is the most important way in which an abridged dictionary is different from an unabridged dictionary?

Find an example of each of these types of dictionaries. Write its title and call number.

3. Unabridged Dictionary

   Title:

   Call number:

4. Abridged Dictionary

   Title:

   Call number:

There are several forms of **electronic dictionaries**. Some are on CD ROM, some are pocket-sized electronic dictionaries, and others may be part of a computer word-processing program.

5. Find an electronic dictionary. Write its name.

Information Found on a Dictionary Page **10-3**

Read the descriptions of the many types of information found on a dictionary page.

1. *Guide words.* There are two guide words at the top of every dictionary page. The first guide word is called the *opening guide word* and tells the first word on the page. The second guide word is called the *closing guide word* and tells the last word on the page.
2. *Entry words.* These are the words listed and defined on the dictionary page. They appear in darker or bolder type on the dictionary page.
3. *Phonetic respelling.* After each entry word you will see a respelling for that entry. The respelling often uses different letters and symbols to show you how to pronounce the word. If you do not know what the letters or symbols mean, look at the *short pronunciation key* found at the bottom of every right-hand page.
4. *Part of speech.* Usually following the respelling you will find an abbreviation that tells the part of speech of the entry. Here are the abbreviations for the common parts of speech:

n = noun	pron = pronoun
v = verb	adv = adverb
adj = adjective	prep = preposition

5. *Definitions.* The definitions for each entry word are presented. The definitions are numbered to show the order of their common use. The most commonly used definition appears first, following the number 1. The next most common definition is numbered 2, and so on.
6. *Variants of the word.* Different forms of the word may also be presented as part of the entry. For example, for the word *define* you may also find the variants *defined* and *defining.*
7. *Origin or etymology.* In some dictionaries you will also find information that tells you where the word came from. For example, the letter *G* might be used to show that the word came from the Greek language, or *L* to show that it has a Latin origin.
8. *Correct usage in a sentence.* Sometimes a sentence containing the entry word is provided. The sentence shows how the word is used in a sentence. For example, to illustrate the meaning of the word *enforce,* the following sentence might be provided:

   A police officer must *enforce* the law.

9. *Synonym or antonym.* Sometimes following the abbreviation *syn* a synonym for the entry word is provided. Sometimes following *ant* an antonym is provided.
10. *Illustration.* Sometimes drawings, pictures, or other types of visuals are presented to illustrate the word.
11. *Short pronunciation key.* This key to the pronunciation of words is usually found at the bottom of every right-hand page. The short pronunciation key contains letters, symbols, and words that will help you pronounce entries you do not know how to say. If the short pronunciation key does not help you pronounce an entry, then look at the long pronunciation key located in the front of your dictionary.

Look at the sample entry from a dictionary page. In each box, place the number for it's description.

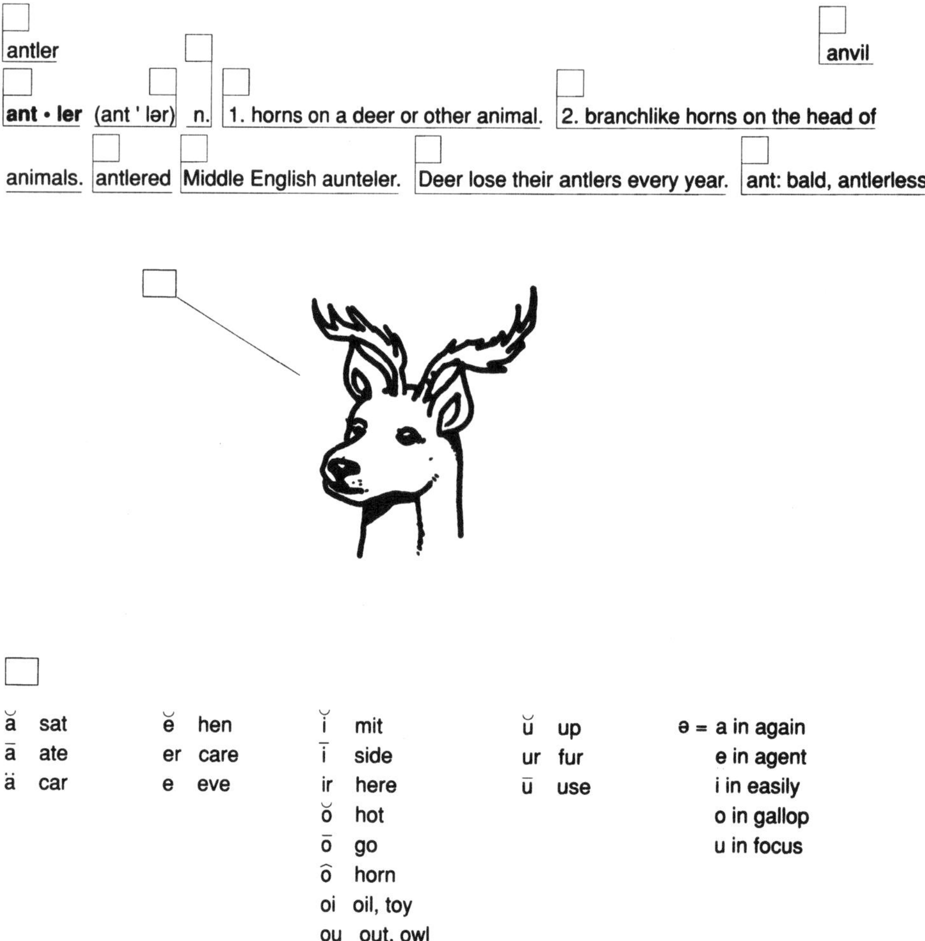

Putting Words in Alphabetical Order 10-4

Words in a dictionary are listed in alphabetical order. The better you are at alphabetizing, the faster you can find words in a dictionary. See how quickly you can write each set of words in alphabetical order.

1. party

   pond

   playground

   piano

2. inside

   itch

   idea

   icicle

3. cough

   cotton

   cover

   cost

4. soot

   song

   soul

   sore

5. fountain

   form

   forward

   fort

6. nice

   nine

   niece

   night

Using Guide Words in a Dictionary **10-5**

At the top of each page in a dictionary you will find a pair of guide words. The first is called the **opening guide word** and is the first entry word listed and defined on that dictionary page. The second is called the **closing guide word** and is the last entry word listed and defined on that page. All the entry words that appear on that dictionary page are in alphabetical order, beginning with the opening guide word and ending with the closing guide word.

Here are three sets of entry words. For each entry word, write the letter that shows the pair of guide words you would use to find it.

Entry Word	*Opening Guide Word*	*Closing Guide Word*
	Set One	
1. _______ cool	a. compare	compete
2. _______ cold	b. coin	come
3. _______ compass	c. cook	copper
	Set Two	
1. _______ hijack	a. hibernation	hideous
2. _______ hitch	b. high	him
3. _______ hickory	c. history	hive
	Set Three	
1. _______ salmon	a. safe	sail
2. _______ sage	b. sardine	satellite
3. _______ sash	c. sale	salt

Phonetic Respellings in a Dictionary

10-6

Phonetic (fə nĕt′ ik) respellings are used in a dictionary to help you pronounce a word. The phonetic respelling follows the entry word on the dictionary page. When you do not know how to pronounce a word, use the phonetic respelling along with the short pronunciation key to pronounce the word. Usually the short pronunciation key is found at the bottom of each right-hand page in the dictionary. If you still cannot pronounce the word, try using the phonetic respelling along with the long pronunciation key, which is found at the front of the dictionary.

Use your dictionary to find the phonetic respelling for each of the following words. Write the phonetic respelling for each word. Use the phonetic respelling and either the short or long pronunciation key found in your dictionary to pronounce each word.

pneumonia

reign

chamber

delinquent

muscle

fugitive

cough

feisty

sophomore

wrinkle

Choosing the Correct Definition

10-7

Many words in the English language have more than one meaning. This is why many entry words are followed by more than one definition. Each definition is numbered to separate it from the others. The first definition is the most commonly used meaning of the word, and the last definition is the least commonly used.

Read each sentence and think about what the highlighted word means in the sentence. Then read the definitions for the highlighted word. Use the meaning of the sentence to help you decide which definition best fits the sentence. Write the definition that best fits the meaning of the sentence.

1. The *palm* broke as I pulled on the oar.
palm (päm) n. 1. bottom part of hand. 2. part of animal forefoot. 3. part of a glove. 4. blade of an oar. 5. linear measure 7–10 inches. 6. to conceal. 7. to pick up stealthily.

____

2. The policewoman gave the driver a *summons* for driving through the red light.
summons (sŭm′ ənz) n. 1. a call to attend a meeting. 2. an official order to appear in court. 3. a traffic ticket.

____

3. Before leaving for the trip we placed our *dunnage* in the trunk of the car.
dunnage (dŭn′ ĭj) n. 1. baggage or personal items. 2. loose material wedged between objects. 3. a cover.

____

4. Mary went on an *odyssey* around the world.
odyssey (ŏd′ ĭ sē) n. 1. a trip characterized by wandering. 2. poem attributed to Homer. 3. a dream.

____

5. Sir Henry is the *Grand* Duke of Windsor.
grand (grănd) adj. 1. standing out in size and beauty. 2. costly. 3. higher in rank than others. 4. amount of money.

____

Learning about Print and Electronic Encyclopedias

10-8

An **encyclopedia** contains articles on a variety of subjects written by experts. The articles are arranged in alphabetical order by topic. There are four types of encyclopedias you should know about. Encyclopedias are available in print and electronic format.

General encyclopedias include overview articles on a wide range of topics. The articles are arranged alphabetically in a set of volumes. Illustrations are also included. The last volume in the set is the index. Information is kept up to date with articles published in yearbooks or supplements. An example of a general encyclopedia is the *Encyclopedia Americana.*

Single-volume encyclopedias include short articles arranged in alphabetical order. There is no index or table of contents. An example of a single volume encyclopedia is the *Random House Encyclopedia.*

Encyclopedias for children and young adults are general encyclopedias for a specific age group. There are many illustrations and study aids, and they are easier to read than other encyclopedias. An example of an encyclopedia for children and young adults is the *World Book Encyclopedia.*

Subject encyclopedias are found for many subjects, such as geography, science, and art. Some are written for adults and others are written for younger students. Articles in a subject encyclopedia are longer, more complete, and more technical than those found in general encyclopedias. An example of a subject encyclopedia is the *World Nature Encyclopedia.*

1. When would you look up your topic in a subject encyclopedia?
2. What kind of encyclopedia would have many pictures?
3. What kind of encyclopedia contains many volumes and includes overview articles on a wide range of different topics?
4. What is not included with a single-volume encyclopedia?

Electronic encyclopedias may be CD ROM with the full text but without pictures; multimedia CD ROM with pictures, video, and sound; or on the World Wide Web. An example of a multimedia encyclopedia is the *Encarta Encyclopedia.*

5. What are three kinds of electronic encyclopedias?

Using Print and Electronic Encyclopedias **10-9**

Encyclopedias are found in either print or electronic form. Find an example of each of the following types of encyclopedias. Write its title and call number. Then √ "Print" or "Electronic" to show the format of the encyclopedia that you found.

General Encyclopedia

Title

Call number

Print _____ Electronic _____

Encyclopedia for Children and Young Adults

Title

Call number

Print _____ Electronic _____

Subject Encyclopedia

Title

Call number

Print _____ Electronic _____

Single-Volume Encyclopedia

Title

Call number

Print _____ Electronic _____

Understanding an Encyclopedia Index Entry

10-10

When you look for information in an encyclopedia, begin by using the index, which is usually located in the last volume. Then select the most important word in your topic. This word is your **keyword.** Look up your keyword in the index. If you cannot find your keyword in the index, select another word in the topic as your keyword.

Using the keyword *endangered* from the topic "Endangered animals in the United States," you might find the following index entry. Study this sample index entry and answer the questions.

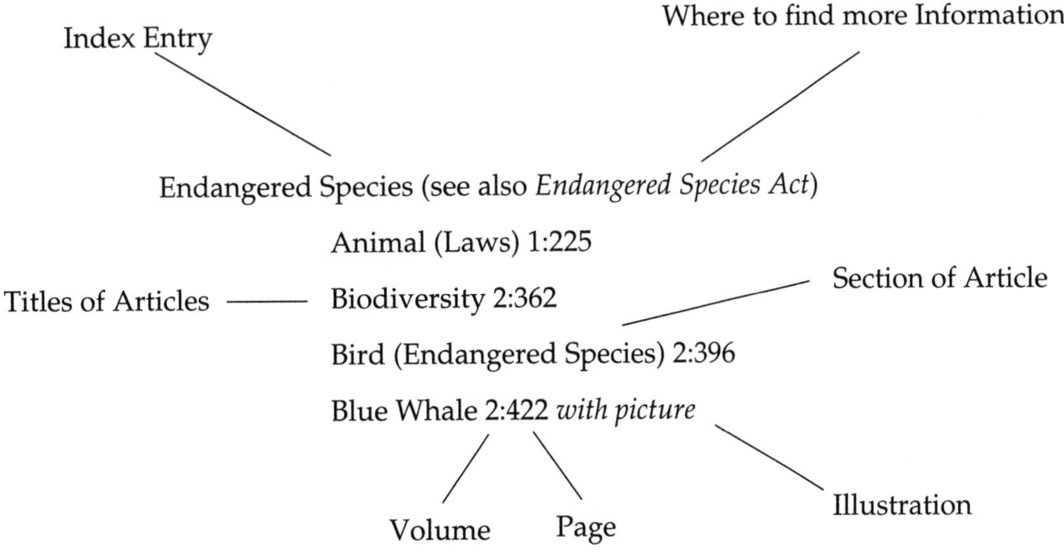

1. In what articles will you find information about the topic?

2. In the article "Animal," under what section will you find information about the topic?

3. In what volume number and on what page will you find the information about endangered birds?

4. In what volume and on what page will you find a picture?

5. Where would you look for more information about the topic?

Using a Thesaurus **10-11**

A **thesaurus** (thĭ sôr′ əs) is a reference book that contains synonyms for commonly used words. The entry words are organized in alphabetical order. Following each entry word is its part of speech and a list of synonyms.

You can use a thesaurus to select words that help you precisely express your ideas when you are writing. Read the following to see how synonyms change the meaning of the sentence.

He *took* the pencil from me.
He *grabbed* the pencil from me.

A **thesaurus** is different from a **dictionary.** A thesaurus contains a large number of synonyms for each entry word. It also gives the part of speech for each synonym. Unlike a dictionary, it does not contain phonetic respellings, definitions, variants of the word, origins of the word, correct usage in sentences, antonyms, or illustrations. A thesaurus contains many more synonyms for commonly used words than does a dictionary. However, a dictionary contains a greater variety of information about each word.

Look at the sample entry for the word *raw* found in a thesaurus. It shows the entry word, part of speech, and a number of synonyms that can be used in place of the entry word.

raw adj. uncooked, crude, inexperienced, rude, coarse, obscene.

For each of the following sentences, use a thesaurus to find a synonym that you can use in place of the highlighted word. Select the synonym that most precisely expresses the idea of the sentence. Write the synonym next to the sentence.

1. The thief *snatched* the purse from the woman.
2. The construction worker was *weary* from a long day at work.
3. The coach was quick to point out the *mistake* made by the player.
4. The main *point* in the newspaper article was the need for more schools.
5. The doctor was *occupied* writing a prescription.
6. He *located* his notebook under a pile of clothes.
7. Manny had a *fantastic* time at the concert.

Practice Using Synonyms **10-12**

Read the following two sentences.

Did you see Joe *eat* the food?
Did you see Tom *devour* the food?

Notice how using the synonym *devour* instead of *eat* in the second sentence changes the meaning of the sentence. Although both *eat* and *devour* have the same general meaning, each has its own specific meaning. The word *eat* suggests consuming food in a slow and orderly manner using a knife and fork. The word *devour* suggests consuming food rapidly using one's hands to rip the food into pieces. Joe eats his food. Tim devours his food.

Read the following pairs of sentences. The first sentence has a highlighted word. In the second sentence the highlighted word has been replaced with a synonym found in a thesaurus. Read the two sentences and explain how the meaning of the first sentence has been changed. You may need to use a dictionary to look up the definitions of some the words.

1. The teacher and the student were involved in an *argument.*
The teacher and the student were involved in a *debate.*

2. The policeman *interrupted* the bank robbery.
The policeman *foiled* the bank robbery.

3. The girl was *eager* to complete her homework.
The girl was *anxious* to complete her homework.

4. The boy *requested* that the new student join them.
The boy *insisted* that the new student join them.

5. The man *explained* the new rules to his employees.
The man *defended* the new rules to his employees.

Using an Almanac **10-13**

An **almanac** is a single-volume reference book containing facts, data, charts, lists, and other methods of organizing useful information. Almanacs provide information about a wide range of topics. They are revised each year so that the information is current. Some frequently used almanacs are:

Information Please Almanac
New York Public Library Desk Reference
Universal Almanac
World Almanac and Book of Facts

Use one of the almanacs listed above or any other almanac to answer the questions. Write the answer to each question and the title of the almanac used to answer the question. Also write the page number(s) where the information needed to answer the question appears in the almanac.

1. How many farms are there in the United States?

Answer:

Title of Almanac:

Page(s):

2. What is the language spoken by the most people in the world? How many people speak it?

Answers:

Title of Almanac:

Page(s):

3. What is the busiest passenger airport in the United States? In the world? Which of these airports is busier?

Answers:

Title of Almanac:

Page(s):

Using an Atlas 10-14

An **atlas** is a collection of maps. Atlases contain maps showing physical and political features of countries throughout the world. Many atlases include sections of maps on specific topics such as climate, population, and agriculture. Some atlases contain maps that portray an event or show how something developed or changed in history.

Two common atlases are:

Hammond Atlas of the World
Times Atlas of World History

Use an atlas to answer the questions. You may have to use more than one atlas to find an answer. Write the answer to each question and the title of the atlas(es) containing the information needed to answer the question. Also write the page number(s) where the information appears in each atlas.

1. What are the names of three countries in Africa?

Answer:

Title(s) of Atlas(es):

Page(s):

2. What is the name of a desert in Australia?

Answer:

Title(s) of Atlas(es):

Page(s):

3. Find a map that shows the population of a place. It can be a city, state, or country. What is the name of this place and its population?

Answer:

Title(s) of Atlas(es):

Page(s):

Using Biographical Sources of Information

10-15

Biographical sources provide information about the lives and accomplishments of famous people, living or dead. Here are some common biographical sources.

Something about the Author	Websters Biographical Dictionary
Dictionary of Scientific Biography	Grolier Library of North American Biographies

Use one of the biographical sources listed above, or any other biographical source in your library, to find information about the famous people listed below. Next to each, write the title of the biographical source containing information about that person. Also write the page number(s) where the information appears. If there is a volume number, write that, too.

Title of Biographical Source Volume/Page(s)

George Washington Carver

Albert Einstein

Sally Ride

Ponce de Leon

Louisa May Alcott

Mark Twain

Winston Churchill

Harriet Tubman

Sandra Day O'Connor

Stephen Crane

Chapter Ten Mastery Assessment

10-16

See what you have learned about using reference sources.

1. What are the five most frequently used types of reference sources?

2. What is an unabridged dictionary?

3. What are entry words?

4. What is a closing guide word on a dictionary page?

5. For what purpose would you use the phonetic respelling of a word in the dictionary?

6. What are the four types of encyclopedias you should know about?

7. What is a keyword?

8. What is a thesaurus?

9. What is an almanac?

10. What is an atlas?

11. What are biographical sources?

ANSWERS FOR CHAPTER TEN REPRODUCIBLE ACTIVITIES

10-1 1. To find background information on a topic, to find facts, and to get a quick answer to a question. 2. Dictionaries, encyclopedias, thesauruses, almanacs, and atlases. 3. Librarian. 4. Answers will vary. 5. Images, sound, video, and animation. 6. Reference sources that do not include images, sound, video, and animation.

10-2 1. Unabridged dictionary. 2. Omits words that are not frequently used. 3. Answers will vary. 4. Answers will vary. 5. Answers will vary.

10-3

[1] antler [1] anvil

[4]

[2] **ant • ler** [3] (ant ' lər) n. [5] 1. horns on a deer or other animal. [5] 2. branchlike horns on the head of animals. [6] antlered [7] Middle English aunteler. [8] Deer lose their antlers every year. [9] ant: bald, antlerless.

[11]

ă	sat	ĕ	hen	ĭ	mit	ŭ	up	ə = a in again
ā	ate	er	care	ī	side	ur	fur	e in agent
ä	car	e	eve	ir	here	ū	use	i in easily
				ŏ	hot			o in gallop
				ō	go			u in focus
				ô	horn			
				oi	oil, toy			
				ou	out, owl			

10-4 1. party, piano, playground, pond. 2. icicle, idea, inside, itch. 3. cost, cotton, cough, cover. 4. song, soot, sore, soul. 5. form, fort, forward, fountain. 6. nice, niece, night, nine.

10-5 Set One. 1. C. 2. B. 3. A. Set Two. 1. B. 2. C. 3. A. Set Three. 1. C. 2. A. 3. B.

10-6 Answers will vary with dictionary used by student.

10-7 1. blade of an oar. 2. a traffic ticket. 3. baggage or personal items. 4. a trip characterized by wandering. 5. higher in rank than others.

10-8 1. When you want to find articles that are longer, more complete, and more technical than those found in general encyclopedias. 2. Encyclopedias for children and young adults. 3. General encyclopedias. 4. Index and table of contents. 5. CD ROM with the full text but without pictures; multimedia CD ROM with pictures, video, and sound; or on the World Wide Web.

10-9 Answers will vary.

10-10 1. Animal; Biodiversity; Bird; Blue Whale. 2. Laws. 3. Volume 2, page 396. 4. Volume 2, page 422. 5. Endangered Species Act.

10-11 Answers will vary.

10-12 Answers will vary.

10-13 Answers will vary.

10-14 Answers will vary.

10-15 Answers will vary.

10-16 1. Dictionaries, encyclopedias, thesauruses, almanacs, and atlases. 2. A dictionary that attempts to include all words currently in use in a language. 3. The words listed and defined on a dictionary page. 4. The last entry word listed and defined on a dictionary page. 5. To learn how to pronounce the word. 6. General, single-volume, encyclopedia for children and young adults, and subject. 7. The main or most important word in a topic. 8. A reference book that contains synonyms for commonly used words. 9. A single volume reference book containing facts, data, charts, lists, and other methods of organizing information. 10. A collection of maps. 11. Reference books providing information about the lives and accomplishments of famous people, living or dead.

CHAPTER ELEVEN

Writing a Research Paper

CHAPTER OBJECTIVES

1. **Teach students a strategy for organizing and writing a research paper.**
2. **Teach students how to identify, locate, and document information needed to write a research paper.**

TITLES OF REPRODUCIBLE ACTIVITIES

11-1 Preparing a Research Paper
11-2 Choosing a Topic
11-3 Knowing If You Have Chosen a Good Topic
11-4 Locating Sources of Information
11-5 Preparing Bibliography Cards
11-6 Bibliography Cards for Electronic Sources
11-7 Bibliography Cards for Internet Sources
11-8 Preparing Note Cards
11-9 Writing an Outline for a Research Paper
11-10 Writing the Research Paper
11-11 Preparing a Bibliography
11-12 Preparing a Title Page
11-13 Preparing a Table of Contents
11-14 Final Checklist
11-15 Chapter Eleven Mastery Assessment

SUGGESTIONS FOR USING THE REPRODUCIBLE ACTIVITIES

After you have distributed a reproducible activity, here are suggestions for its use. Feel free to add further information, illustrations,, or examples. Wherever possible, relate the activity to actual subject area assignments.

11-1 Preparing a Research Paper

Use the activities in this chapter to take students through the steps of writing of a research paper. Students should organize and write their papers as they move through the activities.

Use 11-1 to explain the ten steps in writing a research paper. Have students use the space below each step to record notes.

11-2 Choosing a Topic

Use the introductory text to explain the difference between topics that are either too broad or too narrow and those that are suitable. Use the activity to provide students with practice identifying topics as too broad, too narrow, or suitable.

11-3 Knowing If You Have Chosen a Good Topic

On a separate piece of paper, have students answer the four questions for the topics they wrote. Then have students choose one of their approved topics for their research papers. Have students explain why they chose their topics.

11-4 Locating Sources of Information

Use this activity to familiarize students with the process of getting information from various sources. Students learned about these sources of information in Chapters Eight, Nine, and Ten. If necessary, quickly review these sources. Students will have to go to the library to complete this activity. Encourage them to look for electronic sources of information such as on the Internet or on CD ROM.

11-5 Preparing Bibliography Cards
11-6 Bibliography Cards for Electronic Sources
11-7 Bibliography Cards for Internet Sources

Explain the importance of using bibliography cards to document sources of information used when writing research papers. Tell students they must prepare a separate bibliography card for each source of information they use, whether print or electronic. Use the sample bibliography cards to show how bibliography cards are prepared for various types of sources of information. Point out citations may not always include all the parts called for on a bibliography card. For example, the author might not be identified.

Describe the information found on each card and how the information is presented. Point out that information found on electronic sources is a computer record. The headings on a computer record may not be the same headings as those required for a bibliography card. When this occurs, help students find the information on the computer record that corresponds to the headings on the bibliography card.

Have students prepare bibliography cards for the six types of sources of information found in 11-4. After students have completed 11-5 through 11-7, have them locate additional sources of information they need to write their papers and prepare bibliography cards for these additional sources.

11-8 Preparing Note Cards

Explain to students why they need to prepare note cards. Use the introductory text to guide students through alphabetizing and numbering their bibliography cards. Point out that articles such as *the, a,* and *an* should not be considered the first word when alphabetizing.

Then explain how note cards are prepared and numbered. Emphasize the need for legible writing. Review the sample bibliography card and its note card and have students answer the questions. Then have students prepare note cards for all their bibliography cards.

11-9 Writing an Outline for a Research Paper

Use the introductory text and the sample outline to explain how to write an outline. Direct students to answer the questions. Then have students organize their notes from their note cards and write the outline for their papers.

11-10 Writing the Research Paper

Use the text to explain to students how to write the rough draft of their papers. Help students understand the information that belongs in each section of the paper: introduction, body, and conclusion. Show students how to use the Revising Checklist to improve their rough draft.

11-11 Preparing a Bibliography

Students need to know that a bibliography is an alphabetical list of all the sources of information they used to write their research papers. Use the introductory text to explain how a bibliography is prepared. Then have students prepare the bibliography for their papers using their bibliography cards.

11-12 Preparing a Title Page

Use the introductory text and sample title page to explain how to prepare a title page. Have students answer the question. Then have students prepare a title page for their research papers.

11-13 Preparing a Table of Contents

Use the introductory text and sample table of contents to explain how to prepare a table of contents. Have students use the information provided to prepare a table of contents. Then have them prepare a table of contents for their research papers.

11-14 Final Checklist

Show students how to use the Final Checklist to be sure their research papers are in the correct form to hand in to teachers.

11-15 Chapter Eleven Mastery Assessment

Have students complete this assessment at any point you feel they have learned the ten steps in writing a research paper. Review the results of the assessment with the students. Provide additional instruction as necessary.

Preparing a Research Paper — 11-1

Here are the steps to follow to write a research paper. As your teacher discusses each step, write down the important things you need to remember about each step.

Step 1: Choosing a topic

Step 2: Locating sources of information

Step 3: Preparing bibliography cards

Step 4: Preparing note cards

Step 5: Writing the outline

Step 6: Wring the paper

Step 7: Preparing a bibliography

Step 8: Preparing a title page

Step 9: Preparing a table of contents

Step 10: Final checklist

Choosing a Topic **11-2**

The first step in writing a research paper is to choose a topic. Your topic should not be too broad or too narrow. If your topic is too broad, you will not be able to complete the research paper in the number of pages assigned by your teacher. If your topic is too narrow, you will not find enough information. Be sure to select a topic in which you are interested.

Read each of the following topics. One is too broad, one is too narrow, and the other is suitable. Read to learn why.

The effects of pollution on the lives of people throughout the world.

This topic is too broad because there is too much information on people who live in every country in the world.

The effects of pollution on mallard ducks.

This topic is too narrow because it is limited only to mallard ducks. Although there may be a lot of information available on pollution, there is probably very little on how pollution affects mallard ducks.

The effects of pollution on people who get their water from the Great Lakes.

This topic is suitable for a research paper. The topic is limited to water pollution and to the Great Lakes. There will be enough, but not too much information in your library on this topic.

Read each of the following topics. For each, tell if it is too broad, too narrow, or suitable. Explain your answer.

1. Agriculture in America ____________________

____

2. Raising soybeans in southwest Arkansas ____________________

____

3. Soybean production in the United States ____________________

____

4. The uses of computers ____________________

____

5. Using computers to learn to spell the names of state capitals ____________________

____

6. Using the computer to improve spelling skill ____________________

____

Knowing If You Have Chosen a Good Topic **11-3**

Here are some important questions you should answer about any topic you choose. These questions will help you know if the topic you have chosen is a good one.

Write at least two topics about which you would like to write a research paper.

Topic One. ______________________________

Topic Two. ______________________________

Topic Three. ______________________________

For each topic, answer questions 1–4 on a separate piece of paper.

1. Is the topic too broad, too narrow, or suitable?
   Remember, if the topic is too broad or too narrow, you will find it difficult to complete the paper as required by your teacher.

2. Does your library have enough information available to you on the topic?
   Check in the library to see if there are sufficient numbers of sources of information on the topic. Make sure you have at least as many sources as required by your teacher.

3. Are you interested in the topic?
   Be sure to select a topic in which you are interested. It takes a lot of time to do the research and writing. If you are not interested in the topic, you will probably not do a very good job of writing the paper.

4. Will your teacher approve the topic?
   Show your written topic to your teacher and ask for approval. Do not begin to work on a topic unless your teacher has approved it.

5. Choose one of the topics approved by your teacher for your research paper. Write it here.

6. Why did you choose this topic?

Locating Sources of Information 11-4

For the topic you selected in 11-3, find information on your topic in each of the following sources. For each source, write its title and call number. Check (√) whether it is in print or electronic format. Try to include at least one source that is in electronic format.

Encyclopedia

Title:

Call Number: Print _____ Electronic _____

Other Reference Book

Title:

Call Number: Print _____ Electronic _____

Magazine

Title:

Call Number: Print _____ Electronic _____

Newspaper

Title:

Call Number: Print _____ Electronic _____

Book

Title:

Call Number: Print _____ Electronic _____

Internet

Title of information found:

URL (address):

Preparing Bibliography Cards

11-5

Bibliography cards document sources of information used when writing research papers. Examine the sample bibliography cards prepared for four basic sources of information.

Reference Book

"Water Pollution."
New Times Encyclopedia.
12th ed. 1996.

Magazine Article

Rockman, Julie. "Examining
the Shores of the Great Lakes."
Preserving Mother Nature
28 Oct. 1996: 3-6.

Newspaper Article

"Pollutants Destroying the Great
Lakes."
Detroit Gazette 14 Oct. 1995: 5.

Book

Hanson, Tom. Water Pollution.
Great Falls, Iowa: Appleton
Press, 1996.

Refer to the sample bibliography cards on the previous page to help you prepare bibliography cards for each source of information.

Reference book article entitled, "Polluting America's Great Lakes." found on pages 45–46 of the 14th edition of the World Encyclopedia, 1995.

Magazine article entitled, "Stop Polluting My Drinking Water." Francis Duda is the author. The article appeared in the Great Lakes Monthly Magazine on page 44 of the September 25, 1995, issue.

Book entitled Water All Around Us. Jake Brown is the author. University of Michigan Press, Lansing, Michigan, is the publisher. Published in 1996.

Newspaper article entitled "What I saw on the Beach Made Me Sick" found on page B24 of the Minneapolis Times on October 1, 1995.

Bibliography Cards for Electronic Sources

11-6

Examine the sample bibliography card for an electronic source of information. Headings are provided for the information shown on the card.

Author(s):	Hughes, Patrick.
Title of Article:	"The View from Space."
Title of Publication:	Weatherwise
Date of Article/Page(s):	Jun/Jul 1995: 60–62.
Title of Database:	SIRS Researcher.
Publication Medium:	CD ROM.
Name of Vendor:	SIRS, Inc.,
Date of CD ROM:	1996.

The example provided is for an article from a magazine on CD ROM. You may also find articles from newspapers and encyclopedias on CD ROM. Refer to the sample bibliography card to prepare a bibliography card for the electronic source of information that follows.

Magazine article entitled "Reinventing the Automobile." Christopher Flavin and Nicholas Lenssen are the authors. The article appeared in Solar Today on pages 21–24, in the January–February 1995 issue. The 1996 disc for SIRS Researcher on CD ROM was used. SIRS, Inc. is the name of the vendor.

Author(s):	
Title of Article:	
Title of Publication:	
Date of Article/Page(s):	
Title of Database:	
Publication Medium:	
Name of Vendor:	
Date of CD ROM:	

Bibliography Cards for Internet Sources **11-7**

Examine the sample bibliography card for information found on the Internet. Headings are provided for the information shown on the card.

Author(s):	United States. National Park Service.
Title:	How National Park Units are Established.
Date of Information:	13 Apr. 1995.
Site:	National Park Service.
Address (URL):	http://www.nps.gov/pub_aff/issues/howpark_.html
Online Service:	World Wide Web, Netscape.
Date Accessed:	29 Feb. 1996.

Refer to the sample bibliography card to prepare a bibliography card for the information found on the Internet that follows.

> There is a World Wide Web site called "A Working Hip-Hop Chronology" that can be found at:
>
> http://www.ai.mit.edu/~isbell/HFh/hiphop/rap_history.html

The information was written by Russell A. Potter, Ph.D. (a.k.a. Professa RAP). There is no date given for when this information was written, but it was found online on February 29, 1996, using Netscape Navigator to search the WWW (World Wide Web).

Author(s):

Title:

Date of Information:

Site:

Address (URL):

Online Service:

Date Accessed:

Preparing Note Cards 11-8

Use note cards to record notes from each source you use when writing a research paper. Before you prepare note cards, you must first arrange your bibliography cards in alphabetical order by the first word on the card. Then number all the cards, starting with 1 for the first card. The number should be written in the upper right-hand corner of the bibliography card. Now you are ready to prepare note cards.

When preparing note cards, use two numbers separated by a hyphen. For example, in a note card numbered 4-1, 4 shows that the notes are for the source listed on bibliography card 4, and -1 shows that this is the first card used to record notes from this source. If you need more than one note card to record notes from this source, the second card would be numbered 4-2, and so on for as many note cards as you need. The number of the note card should be written in the upper right-hand corner of the note card. Circle the number to keep it separate from other numbers you might write when taking notes.

Write notes in your own words whenever possible, using abbreviations. Place quotation marks around all quotes. Write the page number on which each quote appears. Look at the following bibliography card and a note card that goes with it.

Bibliography Card

```
Baxson, Bill. Can't Drink the Water or Eat the Fish.        4
South Bend, Indiana: Dwag Press, 1996.
```

Note Card

```
"The water contains mercury and other chemicals." p. 23
Many fish are dying.
Fishing indus hurting & people are worried about their jobs.
New, tough laws are making things better.
Lakes will be safe again soon.
```

1. What do you use to arrange your bibliography cards in alphabetical order?
2. Where do you write the number of a bibliography card?
3. Can a bibliography card have more than one note card?
4. When should you use quotation marks on a note card?
5. Why is the number 4-2 circled on the note card?
6. What does 4 tell you?
7. What does the -2 tell you?

Writing an Outline for a Research Paper **11-9**

To write an outline for a research paper, begin by organizing notes from your note cards into main topics, subtopics, details, and subdetails. Next write the title of the paper near the top of a blank piece of paper. Then, as shown in the sample outline below, write the Roman numeral I and after it the first main topic. Use capital letters before each subtopic that goes with the main topic. Use Arabic numerals before each detail that goes with the subtopic. Use small letters before each subdetail that goes with the detail. Repeat this for each main topic until you have completed the outline. You can write the main topics, subtopics, details, and subdetails as sentences, phrases, or single words.

Examine this sample outline that is labelled for you and answer the questions.

```
Title

  The Effects of Pollution on People Who Get Their Water from the Great Lakes

Main Topic     I. Water for drinking
Subtopic          A. Mercury
Subtopic          B. Iron ore
Subtopic          C. Paper industries
Detail               1. Getting the wood to the paper mills
Subdetail               a. truck
Subdetail               b. railroad
Subdetail               c. floating logs down rivers
Detail               2. Chemicals used to make paper
Subtopic          D. Tourists add to the problem
Main Topic    II. Fish for eating
Subtopic          A. Chemical contamination
Subtopic          B. Fewer fish
Subtopic          C. Takes years to reproduce
Main Topic   III. Recreation
Subtopic          A. There will be less fun in the sun if something isn't done soon.
Subtopic          B. Recreational boaters cause some of the problem.
Subtopic          C. People are scared to swim in the water.
```

1. How should you begin preparing an outline for a research paper?

2. What is the title of this paper?

3. How many subtopics are found for the main topic "Fish for eating?"

4. Write the two details that go with the subtopic "Paper industries."

5. Write the three subdetails that go with this subtopic.

6. Write the main topics.

Writing the Research Paper

11-10

Begin by writing a rough draft of your research paper. Start by writing the title at the top of the page. Then write an introduction that tells the reader what your paper will be about. Use your outline and note cards to write the body of the paper. As you write, insert headings and graphic aids that will help the reader understand your topic. When you have finished writing about your topic, write a conclusion. The conclusion tells the reader what you have learned about the topic or summarizes your point of view. Leave at least one-inch margins on all sides, and double-space the draft to leave room for revising. Number each page in the top right-hand corner as you write.

When you have finished writing a rough draft, examine it to complete the **Revising Checklist.** Place a √ next to each question for which you can answer YES. Revise your draft until you can place a √ next to all the questions.

Revising Checklist

______ 1. Does the introduction clearly introduce the topic?

______ 2. Did I include headings to help the reader understand the topic?

______ 3. Does the body of the paper contain all the facts needed?

______ 4. Does each paragraph contain a main idea?

______ 5. Does every paragraph and sentence add something to the paper?

______ 6. Did I choose the best words to explain my ideas?

______ 7. Does my conclusion follow from the facts?

______ 8. Did I spell all words correctly?

______ 9. Did I capitalize words as needed?

______ 10. Is there subject-verb agreement in all sentences?

______ 11. Are tenses consistent?

______ 12. Are all sentences complete?

______ 13. Did I use quotation marks to identify all quotations?

______ 14. Have I reread the paper several times to find ways to improve it?

______ 15. Did I number the pages correctly?

Preparing a Bibliography

At the end of your research paper you must provide a list of all the sources you used to write your paper. This list of sources is called the **bibliography.** Here is a sample bibliography.

Bibliography

"Covering Up the Pollution Story." Atlanta Daily News 9 Dec. 1995:4.

Frank, Steven. "What Are They Doing to Our Water?" Today's Health Jan. 1995: 62-67.

"Pollution." World Encyclopedia, 1995.

Thompson, Robert. Our Polluted World: What Will We Leave for Our Children? Chicago: Delta Press, 1996.

Thurston, Harry. "The Fatal Shore: The Mystery of Marine Mammal Strandings." Canadian Geographic Jan./Feb. 1995: 60-68. SIRS. CD ROM. SIRS, 1995.

United States Environmental Protection Agency. The Quality of Our Nation's Water.

Environmental Protection Agency. http://www.epa.gov/305b/sum1.html World Wide Web, Netscape Navigator. 5 Mar. 1996.

To prepare a bibliography, you need a blank sheet of paper and your bibliography cards. Write the word "Bibliography" in the center of a line two inches below the top of the sheet of paper. Then check to be sure all your bibliography cards are in alphabetical order by the first word on each card. Now write the information as it appears on each bibliography card. Indent the second and following lines as shown on the sample bibliography above.

On a blank sheet of paper, prepare a bibliography using your bibliography cards.

Preparing a Title Page

The title page is the first page of the research paper. It includes the title of the research paper, the name of the writer, and the date on which the paper is due. To prepare the title page, you need a blank piece of paper. Three inches from the top, write the title using all capital letters. Be sure to center the title. About six inches from the bottom of the sheet of paper and centered, write the word *by*. Two lines below the word *by*, and centered, write your name. Two lines below your name and centered, write the date the paper is due.

Look at a sample title page and answer the question that follows.

SOYBEAN PRODUCTION IN THE UNITED STATES

by

Mary Hardy

January 17, 1997

What information is included on the title page?

Preparing a Table of Contents **11-13**

The table of contents is the second page of the research paper. To prepare the table of contents, you need a blank piece of paper. Three inches from the top and centered, write the words "Table of Contents." Capitalize only the first letter of the word "Table" and the first letter of the word "Contents." Leave a one-inch margin on both the left and right sides of the piece of paper. The table of contents lists the main topics and important subtopics, and the pages on which each is introduced in a research paper. Indent the subtopics. Capitalize the first letter of each major word in each entry in the table of contents. See the sample Table of Contents that follows.

Table of Contents

Now use the following information to prepare a table of contents. Main topics are shown in bold. Subtopics are not bolded.

Introduction, page 1
A land of many trees, page 2
Glorious hardwoods, page 3
Beautiful firs, page 4
Graceful maple trees, page 5
Rapid growth in population, page 6
More housing needed, page 8
Other needs for wood, page 10
Saving the forest, page 12
Conclusion, page 15
Bibliography, page 17

Final Checklist 11-14

When you have finished writing your research paper, examine it to complete the Final Checklist. Place a √ next to each question for which you can answer YES. If you have a √ next to all questions, your paper is ready to be handed in to your teacher. If not, revise your paper until you have a √ next to all questions. Then your paper is ready to be handed in.

Final Checklist

______ 1. Do I have a title page?

______ 2. Do I have a table of contents?

______ 3. Are the pages numbered correctly?

______ 4. Do I have a bibliography?

______ 5. Do I have a second copy for myself?

______ 6. Do I have a folder in which to place the paper to hand in to my instructor?

Chapter Eleven Mastery Assessment **11-15**

See what you have learned about writing a research paper.

1. How many steps must you follow to write a research paper?
2. What problem will you have if you choose a topic that is too broad? Too narrow?
3. List six types of sources that you may use to locate information for your topic.
4. What is the purpose of bibliography cards?
5. On a note card, what does 6-2 mean?
6. Label each part of the following outline:

   I. ______________________________

      A. ______________________________

         1. ______________________________

            a. ______________________________

7. What is the first version of a research paper called?
8. What is a bibliography?
9. What is the first page of the research paper called? The second page?
10. What is the purpose of the Final Checklist?

ANSWERS FOR CHAPTER ELEVEN REPRODUCIBLE ACTIVITIES

11-1 Notes will vary.

11-2 1. Too broad. There are many forms of agriculture in America. 2. Too narrow. Too small a geographical area on which to focus. 3. Suitable. Refers to a specific crop in a sufficiently large geographical area. 4. Too broad. There are many uses of computers. 5. Too narrow. Focuses on too narrow a problem, as there are only fifty capitals whose spelling must be learned. 6. Suitable. Refers to one important skill that can be developed through the use of computers.

11-3 Answers will vary.

11-4 Answers will vary.

11-5 Reference Book

"Polluting America's Great Lakes."
World Encyclopedia
14th ed. 1995.

Magazine Article

Duda, Francis. "Stop Polluting My Drinking Water."
Great Lakes Monthly Magazine
25 Sept. 1995: 44.

Book

Brown, Jake. Water All Around Us.
Lansing, Michigan: University of Michigan Press: 1996.

Newspaper Article

"What I Saw on the Beach Made Me Sick."
Minneapolis Times
1 Oct. 1995: B24.

11-6 Flavin, Christopher and Lenssen, Nicholas.
"Reinventing the Automobile."
Solar Today
Jan./Feb. 1995: 21–24.
SIRS Researcher.
CD ROM.
SIRS, Inc.,
1996.

11-7 Potter, Russell A.
A Working Hip-Hop Chronology.
No Date
A Working Hip-Hop Chronology.
http://www.ai.mit.edu/~isbell/HFh/hiphop/rap_history.html
World Wide Web, Netscape Navigator.
29 Feb. 1996.

11-8 1. First word on the card. 2. Upper-right hand corner. 3. Yes. 4. When you use quotes. 5. To separate it from other numbers you might write when taking notes. 6. The notes are for the source listed on bibliography card 4. 7. It is the second note card used to record notes from the source listed on bibliography card 4.

11-9 1. Organize notes into main topics, subtopics, details, and subdetails. 2. "The Effects of Pollution on People Who Get Their Water from the Great Lakes" 3. Three. 4. Getting the wood to the paper mills; Chemicals used to make paper. 5. truck; railroad; floating logs down rivers. 6. Water for drinking; Fish for eating; Recreation.

11-10 Answers will vary.

11-11 Answers will vary.

11-12 Title of the research paper; name of the writer; date on which the paper is due.

11-13

Table of Contents

11-14 Answers will vary.

11-15 1. Ten. 2. Will find too much information; will not be able to find enough information. 3. Encyclopedia, other reference book; magazine; newspaper; book; Internet. 4. To document sources of information used when writing research papers. 5. Bibliography card 6, note card 2.

6. I. Main Topic
    A. Subtopic
        1. Detail
            a. Subdetail

7. Rough draft. 8. A list of all the sources used to write your paper. 9. Title Page; Table of Contents. 10. To be sure a paper is ready to be handed in.

BIBLIOGRAPHY

Adetumbi, M. (1992). *You're a Better Student Than You Think: A Guide to Memory Improvement, Effective Study Skills, and Motivation for Academic Success*. Huntsville, AL: Adex.

Allen, H. L., Barbe, W. B., & Levesque, T. M. (1996). *Ready-to-use Reading and Study Skills Mastery Activities Secondary Level*. West Nyack, NY: Center for Applied Research in Education.

Amberg, J. (1993). *The Learning Skills Handbook*. Reading, MA: GoodYear-Books.

Barclay, A. (1995). *Teaching Electronic Information Literacy: A How-to-do-it Manual*. New York: Neal-Shuman.

Brescher, A., & Abamont, G. W. (1990). *Study Smart: Ready-to-use Reading/Study Skills Activities for Grades 5–12*. West Nyack, NY: Center for Applied Research Education.

Bromley, K. D., & Irwin-DeVitis, L. (1995). *Graphic Organizers: Visual Strategies for Active Learning*. New York: Scholastic Professional Books.

Cherney, E. E. (1993). *Achieving Academic Success: A Learning Skills Handbook*, 2nd ed. Dubuque, IA: Kendall/Hunt.

Churchill, E. R. (1989). *Tests: How to Study for, Take, and Ace any Test!* Los Angeles: Price/Stern/Sloan.

Clever Kids Study Skills. (1996). Chicago: World Book, Incorporated.

Conan, M., & Heavers, K. (1994). *What You Need to Know about Developing Study Skills, Taking Notes and Tests, Using Dictionaries and Libraries*. Lincolnwood, IL: NTC Publishing Group.

Devine, T. G. (1987). *Teaching Study Skills: A Guide for Teachers*, 2nd ed, Boston: Allyn and Bacon.

Dodge, J. (1994). *Study Skills Handbook: More Than 75 Strategies for Better Learning*. New York: Scholastic.

Fry, R. W. (1996). *How to Study*, 4th ed. Franklin Lakes, NJ: Career Press.

Gall, M. D. (1990). *Tools for Learning: A Guide to Teaching Study Skills*. Alexandria, VA: Association for Supervision and Curriculum Development.

Gayles, Y., & Deloach, A. (1996). *Every Young Person's Guide to Much Better Grades: A Treasury of Study Tips, Tricks, and Secrets for any Student Who Chooses Success*. Chicago, IL: Inner Working Books.

Garrett, L. J., & Moore, J. (1993). *Teaching Library Skills in the Middle and High School: A How-to-do-it Manual*. New York: Neal-Schuman.

Gerber, C. (1992). *Master Study Skills Grade Four*. Columbus, OH: American Education Publishing.

Gerber, C. (1992). *Master Study Skills Grade Five*. Columbus, OH: American Education Publishing.

Gerber, C. (1992). *Master Study Skills Grade Six*. Columbus, OH: American Education Publishing.

Greene, L. J. (1996). *Improving Your Child's Schoolwork: 1,001 Ideas Arranged from A to Z*. Rocklin, CA: Prima.

Greene, L. J. (1993). *Study Smarter, Think Smarter: A Ready-to-Use Study Skills Program for Grades 4–8*. West Nyack, NY: Center for Applied Research in Education.

Herrmann, D. J., Raybeck, D., & Gutman, D. (1993). *Improving Student Memory*. Seattle, WA: Hogrefe and Huber.

Jensen, E. (1996). *Student Success Secrets*, 4th ed. Hauppauge, NY: Barron's Educational Series.

Joyce, M. A., & Tallman, J. I. (1996). *Making the Writing and Research Connection with the I-search Process: A How-to-do-it Manual for Teachers and School Librarians*. New York: Neal-Schuman.

Krantz, H., & Kimmelman, J. (1992). *Keys to Reading and Study Skills*, 4th ed. Fort Worth, TX: Holt, Rinehart and Winston.

MacMillan, J. R., Jr. (1995). *Middle School Success: A Guide to Your Child's Success in Middle School*. Raleigh, NC: JP Press.

Marshall, B., & Ford, W. W. (1994). *The Secrets of Getting Better Grades: Work Smarter Not Harder*. Indianapolis, IN: Park Avenue Publications.

Mastropieri, M. A., & Scruggs, T. E. (1991). *Teaching Students Ways to Remember: Strategies for Learning Mnemonically*. Cambridge, MA: Brookline Books.

McCarthy, M. J. (1990). *Mastering the Information Age: A Course in Working Smarter, Thinking Better, and Learning Faster*. New York: Tarcher.

McInerney, C. F. (1989). *Find It!: The Inside Story at Your Library*. Minneapolis, MN: Lerner Publications.

McPherson, K. R. (1992). *Problem Solving Strategies (Adaptable for Grades 1 through 12)*, 2nd ed., Killeen, TX: McPherson Problem Solving Associates.

Moody, R. B. (1995). *Coming to Terms: Subject Search Strategies in the School Library Media Center*. New York: Neal-Schuman.

Pirozzi, R. C. (1995). *Strategies for Reading and Study Skills*. Lincolnwood, IL: NTC Publishing Group.

Reed, W. (1996). *Study Skills the Key to Student Success*. Dubuque, IA: Kendall/Hunt Publishing Company.

Roach, C., & Moore, J. (1993). *Teaching Library Skills in Grades K through 6: A How-to-do-it Manual*. New York: Neal-Schuman.

Rowntree, D. (1991). *Learn How to Study: A Guide for Students of all Ages*. London: Sphere Books.

Rubin, D. (1992). *Teaching Reading and Study Skills in Content Areas*, 2nd ed. Boston: Allyn and Bacon.

Schumm, J. S., & Radencich, M. C. (1992). *School Power: Strategies for Succeeding in School*. Minneapolis, MN: Free Spirit.

Scruggs, T. E., & Mastropieri, M. A. (1992). *Teaching Test-Taking Skills: Helping Students Show What They Know*. Cambridge, MA: Brookline Books.

Semones, J. K. (1991). *Effective Study Skills: A Step-by-step System for Achieving Student Success*. Fort Worth, TX: Holt, Rinehart and Winston.

Strichart, S. S., & Mangrum, C. T. (1993). *Teaching Study Strategies to Students with Learning Disabilities*. Boston: Allyn and Bacon.

The World Book of Study Power. (1994). Chicago: World Book.

Wirths, C. G., & Bowman-Kruhm, M. (1995). *Upgrade: the High-Tech Road to School Success*. Palo Alto, CA: Davies-Black.

Wooten, S. (1996). *Study Skills: Making the Most of Your Human Computer*. Dubuque, IA: Kendall/Hunt.

MANGRUM-STRICHART LEARNING RESOURCES

Order Form

Study Skills and Strategies Assessment - Grades 4-8 (3S-Gr 4-8)
Special 50% Discount Offer!

Ordering Information:

Schools:	Enclose purchase order number, authorized signature and title.
Individuals:	Orders must be prepaid. Please enclose check or money order.
Teachers:	You may order as an individual or your school will be billed if you provide an approved purchase order number.

Quantity	Item	Regular Price	50% Discounted Price	Subtotal
_____	First 3S-Gr 4-8 disk with 50 administrations	$ 49.95	$ 24.95	_____
_____	Each Additional 3S-Gr 4-8 disk with 50 administrations	$ 29.95	$ 14.95	_____
_____	First 3S-Gr 4-8 disk with unlimited administrations	$109.95	$ 54.95	_____
_____	Each Additional 3S-Gr 4-8 disk with unlimited administrations	$ 79.95	$ 39.95	_____

Florida Residents add 6% Sales Tax........ _____
or include Tax Exempt Number_____________________
Shipping and Handling ($ 4.95 for first disk; $ 1.95 each additional disk)........ _____

Check format desired: Windows____ Macintosh____ **TOTAL ORDER** [ ]
Please write for network license and pricing.

Method of Payment -- check one

- ☐ Check enclosed for _______________
- ☐ Money order enclosed for__________
- ☐ Bill us. Purchase order No.__________
  (Schools Only -- Purchase order with authorized signature and title enclosed)

Send all orders to:

MANGRUM-STRICHART LEARNING RESOURCES
Order Department
9841 SW 122 Street
Miami, FL 33176

Please make check or money order payable to:

MANGRUM-STRICHART LEARNING RESOURCES
prices subject to change

Thank you for your order!

A companion book containing reproducible activities, **Teaching Study Skills and Strategies in Grades 4-8**, is available from: Allyn and Bacon Order Department, P.O. Box 10695, Des Moines, IA 56336-0695 or call 1-800-278-3525.

Ship to: *(Please print)*

Name_______________________
School_______________________
Address_______________________
City_______________________
State__________Zip__________
Telephone No. (_____)__________

Bill to: *(Please print)*

Name_______________________
School_______________________
Address_______________________
City_______________________
State__________Zip__________
Purchase Order No.______________
Telephone No. (_____)__________

LICENSING AGREEMENT

You should carefully read the following terms and conditions before opening this disk package. Opening this disk package indicates your acceptance of these terms and conditions. If you do not agree with them, you should promptly return the package unopened.

Allyn and Bacon provides this Program and License its use. You assume responsibility for the selection of the Program to achieve your intended results, and for the installation, use, and results obtained from the Program. This License extends only to use of the Program in the United States or countries in which the Program is marketed by duly authorized distributors.

License Grant
You hereby accept a nonexclusive, nontransferable, permanent License to install and use the Program on a single computer at any given time. You may copy the Program solely for backup or archival purposes in support of your use of the Program on the single computer. You may not modify, translate, disassemble, decompile, or reverse engineer the Program, in whole or in part.

Term
This License is effective until terminated. Allyn and Bacon reserves the right to terminate this License automatically if any provision of the License is violated. You may terminate the License at any time. To terminate this License, you must return the Program, including documentation, along with a written warranty stating that all copies of the Program in your possession have been returned or destroyed.

Limited Warranty
The Program is provided "As Is" without warranty of any kind, either express or implied, including, but not limited to, the implied warranties or merchantability and fitness for a particular purpose. The entire risk as to the quality and performance of the Program is with you. Should the Program prove defective, you (and not Allyn and Bacon or any authorized distributor) assume the entire cost of all necessary servicing, repair, or correction. No oral or written information or advice given by Allyn and Bacon, its dealers, distributors, or agents shall create a warranty or increase the scope of its warranty.

Some states do not allow the exclusion of implied warranty, so the above exclusion may not apply to you. This warranty gives you specific legal rights and you may also have other rights that vary from state to state.

Allyn and Bacon does not warrant that the functions contained in the Program will meet your requirements or that the operation of the Program will be uninterrupted or error free.

However, Allyn and Bacon warrants the disk(s) on which the Program is furnished to be free from defects in material and workmanship under normal use for a period of ninety (90) days from the date of delivery to you as evidenced by a copy of your receipt.

The Program should not be relied on as the sole basis to solve a problem whose incorrect solution could result in injury to a person or property. If the Program is employed in such a manner, it is at the user's own risk and Allyn and Bacon explicitly disclaims all liability for such misuse.

Limitation of Remedies
Allyn and Bacon's entire liability and your exclusive remedy shall be:

1. The replacement of any disk not meeting Allyn and Bacon's "Limited Warranty" and that is returned to Allyn and Bacon or
2. If Allyn and Bacon is unable to deliver a replacement disk or cassette that is free of defects in materials or workmanship, you may terminate this Agreement by returning the Program.

In no event will Allyn and Bacon be liable to you for any damages, including any lost profits, lost savings, or other incidental or consequential damages arising out of the use or inability to use such Program even if Allyn and Bacon or an authorized distributor has been advised of the possibility of such damages or for any claim by any other party.

Some states do not allow the limitation or exclusion of liability for incidental or consequential damages, so the above limitation or exclusion may not apply to you.

General
You may not sublicense, assign, or transfer the License of the Program. Any attempt to sublicense, assign, or transfer any of the rights, duties, or obligations hereunder is void.

This Agreement will be governed by the laws of the State of Massachusetts.

Should you have any questions concerning this Agreement, or any questions concerning technical support, you may contact Allyn and Bacon by writing to:

Allyn and Bacon
Simon and Schuster Education Group
160 Gould Street
Needham Heights, MA 02194

You acknowledge that you have read this Agreement, understand it, and agree to be bound by its terms and conditions. You further agree that it is the complete and exclusive statement of the Agreement between us that supersedes any proposal or prior Agreement, oral or written, and any other communications between us relating to the subject matter of this Agreement.

Notice to Government End Users
The Program is provided with restricted rights. Use, duplication, or disclosure by the Government is subject to restrictions set forth in subdivision (b)(3)(iii) of The Rights in Technical Data and Computer Software Clause 252.227-7013.